Confirmation

A community preparation

GW01418735

Confirmation
A community preparation

PETER HUMFREY

GEOFFREY CHAPMAN

LONDON

A Geoffrey Chapman book published by
Cassell Publishers Limited
Artillery House, Artillery Row,
London SW1P 1RT
© Peter Humfrey, 1984, 1985

Interim version first published 1984
This edition first published 1985
Reprinted 1988
Reprinted 1989

ISBN 0 225 66472 0

Nihil obstat: Anton Cowan, *Censor*
Imprimatur: Monsignor John Crowley, *V.G.*
          Westminster, 3 July 1985
The *Nihil obstat* and *Imprimatur* are a declaration that a book or
pamphlet is considered to be free from doctrinal or moral error. It is not
implied that those who have granted the *Nihil obstat* and *Imprimatur*
agree with the contents, opinions or statements expressed.

British Library Cataloguing in Publication Data
Humfrey, Peter, 19————
    Confirmation: a community preparation. — 2nd ed.
    1. Confirmation — Catholic Church — study and teaching
    I. Title   II. Humfrey, Peter, 19—————. Community confirmation
    programme.
    265'.2   BX2210

Phototypesetting by Georgia Origination, Liverpool
Printed at The Bath Press, Avon

Contents

Acknowledgements

The publishers would like to thank those concerned for permission to reproduce the following material.

Scripture passages taken from The Jerusalem Bible, published and copyright 1966, 1967 and 1968 by Darton, Longman and Todd Ltd and Doubleday & Co. Inc., and used by permission of the publishers. Excerpts from the English translation of *Rite of Baptism for Children* © 1969, International Committee on English in the Liturgy, Inc. (ICEL); excerpts from the English translation of *The Roman Missal* © 1973, ICEL; excerpts from the English translation of *Rite of Penance* © 1974, ICEL; excerpts from the English translation of *Rite of Confirmation*, Second Edition © 1975, ICEL; ICEL. All rights reserved.

'In bread we bring you, Lord' by Kevin Nichols © Kevin Mayhew Ltd, Rattlesden, Bury St Edmunds, Suffolk IP30 0SZ. All rights reserved. Reprinted by permission.

'Make us worthy, Lord' reproduced by permission of the Co-workers of Mother Teresa.

Drawings from *Developing in Christ*, *Teacher's Handbooks* 1 and 2 © 1981 Pastoral Institute of Eastern Africa.

Photographs by Martin Knops.

Foreword

The preparation of candidates for the Sacrament of Confirmation is a most important part of every parish activity. It is the family of the Church handing on and sharing its Faith with a new generation. As such, as well as the candidates themselves, it involves the active participation of catechists, parents and priests and, indeed, the whole parish community, which helps to welcome and prepare the candidates. This book contains material for discussion, study and prayer, and will be a very helpful tool in this process.

Every catechetical book, to be an effective instrument of Christian formation, must be linked with the real life of the people to whom it is addressed, try to speak a language that is understood by those people, give the whole message of Christ in its exposition of the Church's doctrine, and give those who use the book a better understanding of the mystery of Christ so as to promote a deeper and more generous Christian life.

This book by Fr Peter Humfrey endeavours to do this and I am pleased to commend it. It is based on many years of experience in preparing candidates for the Sacrament of Confirmation and I hope it will be of great assistance to all those involved in the preparation of our Catholic young people.

+ CORMAC

Rt Rev. Cormac Murphy-O'Connor
Bishop of Arundel and Brighton

Introduction

To candidates

Welcome to this new stage of your journey in faith. You have thought about the invitation from God to receive the gift of the Holy Spirit in the sacrament of Confirmation. You will become more fully a member of God's Church and a disciple of Christ.

This book contains ideas to help you explore and discuss your Christian life,

> passages from the word of God which reveal his love and his plan for you,
> some of the teaching of the Church about the Christian life,
> activities to help you deepen your knowledge and love of God and of those around you,
> some ideas on prayer and liturgy to help the community support you at this time in your life.

May God bless you now and always,

To parents, sponsors, catechists and priests

God has called you in your own special way to help those to whom he wishes to give his Spirit in the sacrament of Confirmation. This book is both for the candidates and for you. It will help you to discuss and share your faith with one another.

The candidates may benefit from all the resources in your community. You accompany the candidate as he or she grows in faith on the pilgrim journey in the way of unity and peace.

May God bless your work and your journey,

Peter Humfrey

You will receive power
when the Holy Spirit comes on you,
and then you will be my witnesses
not only in Jerusalem
but throughout Judaea and Samaria,
and indeed to the ends of the earth.
                                    Acts 1:8

What is Confirmation?

Confirmation is one of the sacraments of initiation into the Christian Church. The other two are Baptism and Eucharist. Confirmation as a sacrament of initiation completes Baptism liturgically and initiates the Christian into a more intensified or mature level of discipleship. It is both a gift and an invitation. It evokes a response in the one who listens to God's call.

In infant Baptism the Church calls for a profession of faith and assent from the parents and godparents; in Confirmation the Church calls for a profession of faith and assent from the recipient, supported by the sponsor.

In their own vocation parents draw on the gifts of the Holy Spirit. When the first stages of the religious formation of their children are completed, these too are initiated into a way of life or vocation guided by the gifts of the Spirit.

The act of anointing with chrism and the accompanying words indicate the effect of the sacrament. In the Old Testament, anointing by God's minister originally indicated appointing or commissioning, as with Aaron. Later it involved an inner change, as when Samuel anoints Saul, 'God changed his heart' (1 Samuel 10:9), and David, 'the spirit of the Lord came mightily on David from that day forward' (1 Samuel 16:13).

In the New Testament Jesus is *the* Anointed One, 'God had anointed him with the Holy Spirit and with power' (Acts 10:38). Though the signs at the Jordan at the beginning of his public ministry do not include oil, at Nazareth when Jesus proclaims his mission he quotes from Isaiah to acknowledge that he has been anointed (appointed) for it, and that he has received the Spirit.

The Church today needs to mark, for its growing members, the movement from the vocation of a child toward that of an adult. The Letter to the Ephesians expresses the vocation of the child in the Church: 'Children, be obedient to your parents in the Lord – that is your duty' (Ephesians 6:1). At Confirmation the Church celebrates the adult vocation of the baptised Christian, 'I implore you to lead a life worthy of your vocation' (Ephesians 4:1).

When an infant is baptised the call is issued: 'As Christ was anointed Priest, Prophet and King, so may you live always as a member of his Body'. But now it is not the parents who spell out this vocation, but the Church community led by the Bishop. Confirmation may be called the Christian's initiation into a more mature discipleship in the Church community and the completion of Baptism.

Parents' meetings

Faith is a gift from God. 'You have been saved through faith; not by anything of your own, but by a gift from God' (Ephesians 2:8). Children first meet God through their parents and then through adults who touch their lives. Parents need to have the opportunity to develop their life of faith, that they may continue to grow into more faithful followers of Jesus Christ.

Being a parent is itself a process of development. Parents do not simply pass on faith but are themselves models or examples of faith. They need to meet together to foster their own growth and to develop relationships by sharing beliefs which express their faith.

Not only at Baptism but at other sacramental moments parents continue to meet new problems, crises and challenges. Transformation and growth take place within and through these experiences. The community sharing its faith supports and guides parents in their Christian journey.

We can identify some of the needs of parents:
    to be accepted by those around them,
    to belong to the Christian community,
    to be affirmed in their vision and their aspirations,
    to be valued for their knowledge and experience.

We can identify too some of the tasks of parents:
    to develop as persons and nurturers,
    to reflect on and accept the Christian faith and tradition,
    to share the story of Christianity with their children,
    to foster hopes and dreams for love and justice.

In this programme all parents should have the opportunity to meet comfortably whatever their background or circumstances. They should be asked what kind of support and guidance they would like from the community. This would include meaningful information and support in their own lives as well as an opportunity for active participation in the programme (see page 13). As parents continue to grow in their own faith they will be more able to catechise their children.

Catechists' meetings

Catechists have a particular part to play in the preparation of young people for Confirmation. 'I did the planting, Apollos did the watering, but God made things grow' (1 Corinthians 3:6). Before beginning a programme the catechetical team should meet and discuss some of the following questions:

The vision

Look first at the society in which we live and function as a Church.

What kind of society are we creating?

With which groups of people do we identify and share our vision?

What are the conflicts we face today?

What is our purpose in being Christians in our society?

What is our vision of the role of the Church in today's world?

The strategy

Look at where Confirmation fits into our strategy for the Church.

Why do we have Confirmation?

What are we aiming for in our Confirmation programme?

What is the place of young adults in the Church?

Where does Confirmation fit into the pastoral strategy of our local Church?

The structures

Look at the current practice of the Church.

Why does the Bishop normally confirm?

What criteria do we use for belonging to the Church?

What kind of community are the candidates being initiated into?

What do we understand by the terms 'freedom' and 'commitment'?

What do we understand by the call to be 'disciples of Christ'?

What concern do we show for the minority groups, the unchurched, the spiritually poor and the disillusioned?

The method

Consider what methods are best to bring about what you hope to achieve.

Why should we use the catechumenate model (Rite of Christian Initiation of Adults)?

What is the role of the catechist?

Who will appoint the catechists?

Who will train and support the catechists?

To whom are the catechists responsible?

What is the role of the Catholic school?

Candidates' meetings

This Confirmation programme has been worked out with regard to modern theories of the psychological and educational development of young people. The object of this project is to enable the faith of the participants to grow and develop.

Before adolescence children think in a very concrete way. They take their perspective in life very much from their own point of view. Their judgements about morality are based on material considerations and on a 'fair is fair' attitude. They accept the authority of those who fill authority-roles. They see the world through stories, often in quite dramatic forms. They have a literal view of symbols.

Adolescents think in more formal and abstract ways. They take a great interest in interpersonal relationships. Their moral attitudes reflect their feelings about relationships. They accept the consensus of the groups they value. They respect those who offer them a worthwhile tradition. Their view of the wider world is not often openly and coherently expressed, but nonetheless they feel deeply about world issues. The symbols in their lives have many dimensions and are often very powerful.

Moving towards adulthood, young people become aware of the dichotomies in their thinking. They tend to join the group or class whose outlook on life they find acceptable. The moral judgements they make are relative to such groups. They base their acceptance of authority on their own judgements. They can express their views about the world objectively and in abstract terms. In their own relationships, they are conscious of the links and the boundaries. They can distinguish now between symbols themselves and the meaning they convey.

Clearly, further changes take place in the life of young adults as their faith matures. However, there is no guarantee that this programme will develop a person's faith automatically. These observations about growth simply help us to define where people are in their journey and to respond accordingly.

We may identify some of the needs of young adults:

> to be regarded as complete and whole persons,
> to discover their own personal value systems,
> to develop good personal relationships,
> to build confidence in themselves and their capabilities.

Similarly we may identify some of the tasks of young adults:

> to develop a living, conscious and active faith through knowledge of the Gospel and the traditions of the Church,
> to make a personal search for identity and belonging within the Christian community,
> to become aware of the needs of the community and the world, and respond in a spirit of self-giving,
> to become aware of their calling and become accustomed to giving witness to the hope that is in them.

While participating in a Confirmation programme, candidates will often be in a process of change, upheaval and reorganisation which will lead to a more mature awareness of their own identity. They are putting off concepts and ideas inherited from childhood, which may include parental authority and a childish perception of God. Intellectually they may want to develop a critical stance, even to taking a strong line in an argument. But they will increasingly need to view the world also from others' points of view.

Some young people may not wish to stand out as different in any way or be treated differently. They may experience deep emotions, religious fervour and frequent changes of mind and mood. They may be caught up in situations where emotions are not sufficient to cope; they may not know what to do, but may not be ready to accept help or advice.

Others may be belligerent, ungracious and the cause of embarrassment to parents, family and other adults. They may affect an uncaring attitude and be inarticulate about problems. They may feel misunderstood, uneasy and insecure.

The catechist needs to present the value of order and self-discipline, the coherence and rationality of belief and the rewards to be found in continuing to search for meaning and identity.

The maturity of Christ may be offered as a model to young people. The dignity of the person, his or her work and the use of talents for others' benefit can bring a broader and more settled perspective on life.

Candidates need approval and acceptance, an understanding of their inarticulacy and contradictions, and to be credited with basic sincerity and good will. They must above all have the freedom to respond to Christ in their own way.

A history of Confirmation

A brief survey of the history of the sacrament will show the main theological and pastoral concerns of the Church at different times.

The early Church

In the early Church it was recognised that God's spirit could be poured out on gentiles too (Acts 10:32-48) and they were admitted to full membership in the new Church (Acts 15:5-29). Baptism was the sign that they had accepted the message of Christ and received the Spirit of God. By the year 200 most of the Christian communities had an initiation ritual which included water baptism signifying spiritual regeneration and additional rites signifying reception of the Holy Spirit. By the year 400 baptism, the imposition of hands and anointing variously indicated the gift of the Spirit.

Fourth to eighth centuries

The influx of numerous converts, the rise of infant baptism and the development of missionary baptism in the succeeding centuries meant that bishops were generally unavailable. A variety of different practices ensued. The French Council of Riez in 439 first used the name 'Confirmation'. Bishop Faustus of Riez preached that in baptism the Holy Spirit gave new life but in Confirmation the Spirit gave additional strength needed for the battle with sin and the devil in adulthood. About 850 a group of French clergy put together a document, later called Isidore's False Decretals, which established the practice of priestly baptism and episcopal Confirmation throughout Europe. Raban Maur, abbot of Fulda, wrote that Confirmation gave strength to battle with evil and to witness to the faith.

Ninth to thirteenth centuries

William Durand, bishop of Mende, established the normal practice but also made some changes in the rite. Individual imposition of hands was replaced by collective imposition and the kiss of peace was substituted by a slap. The age of Confirmation rose to the 'age of discretion': that is, from seven to about fourteen.

The scholastic theologians posed five questions about the sacrament: was Confirmation necessary? What was the 'matter and form'? Was it instituted by Christ? What was the 'character' of Confirmation? What was the effect of Confirmation?

The answers to these questions provided the common understanding of Confirmation up to modern times.

Modern times

Twentieth-century historical research led to a reconsideration of the medieval theology. Theologians distinguished between Baptism and Confirmation first by proposing that Baptism gave a dynamic presence of the Spirit and Confirmation the indwelling of the Spirit. Later it was suggested that Baptism gave the indwelling of the Spirit but that Confirmation gave the seven gifts of the Spirit. In the 1940s and 1950s Confirmation was viewed by some as the sacrament of 'Catholic Action'.

With the liturgical movement there returned the notion that Confirmation was the perfection of Baptism and the sign of acceptance not only by the parish but by the diocese and the whole Church represented by the bishop.

In the 1960s theologians spoke of Confirmation as 'a sign of grace', 'a call to live by the power of God's Spirit rather than according to the spirit of the times', 'a celebration of Christian maturity', 'the recognition of personally accepted faith', 'the call to take up responsibility to be disciples of Christ'.

The Second Vatican Council directed that the Rite should be revised to show the close connection with Baptism. In his instruction the bishop reminds the candidates that they are called to be witnesses to Christ and more perfect members of the Church. But they then renew their baptismal promises and the bishop prays that they will be filled with the Holy Spirit. So Confirmation is viewed both as part of Christian initiation and as a separate sacrament with effects of its own.

Of Confirmation the Second Vatican Council says only this: candidates 'are endowed with special strength . . . are bound more intimately to the Church . . . and more strictly obliged to spread and defend the faith both by word and by deed as true witnesses of Christ'.

The debate about the meaning of the sacrament and the best age for its reception continues. The usual age for Confirmation varies from as early as seven to as late as eighteen. Disagreements about the age for Confirmation go hand in hand with disagreements about the meaning of the rite. The liturgically-minded support an early age for Confirmation to show its original liturgical connection with Baptism. The educationally-minded often support a later age so that those baptised in infancy may make a more mature decision to be confirmed in the Church. This delay also provides an opportunity for catechesis not only of the candidate but also of the community within which the Confirmation takes place.

The RCIA and Confirmation

Confirmation is one of the three sacraments of initiation. The Rite of Christian Initiation of Adults (RCIA) is the foundation and model for all catechesis. Our programme is a community project adapted to local needs according to the provisions of the Rite (see Rite no.2).

The initiation of catechumens [candidates] takes place step by step in the midst of the community of the faithful. Together with the catechumens, the faithful reflect upon the value of the paschal mystery, renew their own conversion, and by their example lead the catechumens to obey the Holy Spirit more generously (no.4).

The candidate makes a spiritual journey, stage by stage. The first stage is a time of enquiry and evangelisation. The second stage is a time of growing in faith and understanding. The third stage is a time of deeper spiritual preparation (Lenten retreat). The fourth stage is a time of post-sacramental experience of the life and unity of the community (see nos.8-40).

The first stage is a time of evangelisation: in faith and constancy the living God is proclaimed, as is Jesus Christ, whom he sent for the salvation of men. Thus the hearts of the candidates may be opened by the Holy Spirit, and they may sincerely adhere to him who is the way, the truth and the life, and who fulfils all their spiritual expectations, indeed goes far beyond them (see no.9).

During the second stage the priests and the catechists give the candidates a pastoral formation which leads to a suitable knowledge of dogmas and precepts and also to an intimate understanding of the mystery of salvation. Helped by parents, sponsors, godparents and the whole community, the candidates will learn to pray to God more easily, to witness to the faith, to be constant in the expectations of Christ in all things, to follow supernatural inspiration in their deeds and to exercise charity towards their neighbours to the point of self-renunciation. By suitable liturgical rites, the Church helps the candidates on their journey, cleanses them little by little and strengthens them with God's blessing (see no.19).

After Confirmation, the community and the confirmed move forward together, meditating on the gospel, sharing in the eucharist and performing works of charity. In this way they understand the paschal mystery more fully, and bring it into their lives more and more (no.37). By this frequenting of the sacraments, the knowledge and experience of both candidates and community is increased and developed (see no.39).

Ministries in Confirmation

The parents

The role of the parents is to continue to show the love of Christ for their children in the family, the domestic church; to accompany them sympathetically on their spiritual journey; to answer as they are able the questions and problems of the young person; to give an example of prayer and Christian living and to pray for their child during this time of preparation. By meeting with other parents, they may provide a supportive community of prayer and witness, and in their turn strengthen each other's faith.

The priest

The priest attends to the pastoral and spiritual care of the candidates, especially those who seem hesitant and weak. He celebrates the various liturgies by which the candidates are drawn more deeply into the mystery of Christ. He is responsible for the provision of catechesis with the help of catechists and their helpers.

The catechists

The catechists make an important contribution to the progress of the candidates and the growth of the community. They should have an active part in the liturgies. When teaching, they should see that their instruction is filled with the spirit of the gospel. They should accompany the candidates as guides and helpers on the spiritual journey, and should help the candidates to interpret the signs of the times in the light of the gospel. They should work closely with the priest and the community, sharing the meditation on and explanation of the gospels and the tradition of the Church.

The sponsors

The sponsors represent the community and express in a personal and particular way the responsibilities of the community. The sponsors provide affirmation, encouragement and guidance for the candidate's growth in faith. They engender trust and prove trustworthy in supporting the candidate through any difficulties. They help the candidate to face difficult issues and avoid self-deception. The sponsors and the community should provide models of faith and experience, of education and spiritual direction that deepen and expand the faith of the candidate. The sponsors may be the god-parents or some other suitable people acceptable to the community.

How to use the programme

It is important that candidates are not simply given information about religion without being given the opportunity to experience its meaning and importance for themselves and their own lives. This programme challenges both the intellectual and the spiritual growth of those who take part. It is designed to take place over a period of seven months.

Time of enquiry (Evangelisation)	First month	Theme 1	People of God
	Second month	Theme 2	Advent
LITURGY OF ENROLMENT AS CANDIDATES			
Time of catechesis (Catechumenate)	Third month	Theme 3	Baptism
	Fourth month	Theme 4	Reconciliation
	Fifth month	Theme 5	Eucharist
	Sixth month	Theme 6	Confirmation
CELEBRATION OF CONFIRMATION			
Time of mission (Mystagogia)	Seventh month	Theme 7	Mission

The first two themes presuppose a process of enquiry with no obligation on the part of the candidate at this stage. This may be a time of basic evangelisation rather than catechesis. We begin with *their* questions about God, Jesus and the Church.

After the Enrolment Service, the candidates begin a period of structured and intensive study of the faith. This includes aspects of prayer and daily Christian living within the Christian community.

After Confirmation the newly confirmed meet to consider the next stage of their Christian life and how this can be lived more fully in the light of God's gift of his Spirit.

How to use each theme

Each theme should be prepared first by the catechetical team. The *first meeting* of the month is for parents so they may know and understand what will happen to their children. In this way their own faith will grow and develop.

The *second meeting* of the month is for the candidates with their catechists. This meeting will include the discussion points and the study of the word of God and the teaching of the Church. A long meeting will go on to some of the activities. Otherwise these should be held over to the fourth week.

The *third meeting* of the month will be to celebrate the liturgy. This may be a celebration of the theme at a Sunday Mass or a non-eucharistic celebration at some other suitable time and place. The liturgies should always be adapted to suit the occasion.

The *fourth meeting* of the month is designed to consolidate the previous meetings and develop more clearly the link of each theme with the forthcoming Confirmation. Material held over from previous meetings may be used in addition to the suggested activities.

The four meetings on each theme could be planned as follows:

Week one Wednesday	Meeting for parents and catechists
Week two Wednesday	Meeting for candidates and catechists (Study)
Week three Sunday	Celebration of the liturgy of the theme
Week four Friday	Meeting for candidates and catechists (Activities)

Key ideas

These three points show the important elements of doctrine, witness and prayer for each theme. They may be used as starting points, or to summarise the theme at the end.

Discussion points

These are questions to help reflection on the human experience connected with the theme. The reflection may be introduced by the picture or by the questions in the book or by slides or other photos. Questions will arise about God, Christ and the Church. Ideas should be pooled and shared.

The word of God

Selected passages of scripture are chosen to pinpoint some key ideas which illuminate the human experience of the theme. These passages are by no means exhaustive, but they have been tried and tested in many groups.

The teaching of the Church

The Tradition of the Church is expressed mainly in excerpts from the Second Vatican Council and the more recent teaching of Pope John Paul II. The message is followed by questions designed to provoke deeper reflection.

Activities

The suggestions here will help a deeper appreciation of the consequences of the word of God and the teaching of the Church. They will draw the group more closely together and provide material for more personal reflection.

Prayer and liturgy

The prayers are both ancient and modern. The liturgies, which may be eucharistic or non-eucharistic, consolidate the discussion and study in community prayer and celebration. They should be adapted to local circumstances and needs.

The Confirmation Retreat

The Confirmation Retreat is a most important and valuable way of giving to the candidates an experience of living in a Christian community. It provides an opportunity for learning more deeply about the sacrament and its implications for living a Christian life. It is also the occasion of greater pastoral care of the candidates through counselling, advice and growth in prayer and spirituality.

The team running the Retreat would ideally consist of a priest, a religious, a married couple, some catechists and some young adults. The team should prepare together some time ahead. Care should be taken to choose a suitable environment, to advertise effectively and to help with the cost where necessary.

This is a sample programme:

Theme: 'Receive the Holy Spirit'

Thursday

11.00 Welcome, Introduction and group work

1.00 Lunch

2.30 Session 1: The Good News of Jesus Christ

4.00 Tea

5.00 Prepare for Mass

6.30 Supper

8.00 Mass

9.00 Social gathering, games, etc.

10.00 Night prayer and bedtime.

Friday

8.15 Morning prayer

8.30 Breakfast

9.30 Session 2: The Church in the world today

10.30 Coffee

11.00 Group work

12.30 Lunch

1.30 Outdoor activities

2.30 Session 3: My mission after Confirmation

4.00 Tea

4.30   Desert time – private reflection

5.00   Closing liturgy of strengthening and commissioning

6.00   Departure in peace to love and serve the Lord.

This Retreat may take place early in the programme to help the candidates get to know one another or later when there is greater opportunity for spiritual growth. In any case the chance to follow up the ideas and questions later should not be neglected.

Further reading

The Rite of Christian Initiation of Adults. CTS, 1974
Catechesis in our Time. St Paul, 1979
Evangelisation in the Modern World. CTS, 1976
The New Rite of Penance. Veritas, 1976
Rite of Confirmation. St Paul, 1972
Confirmation: The Rite. CTS, 1973
Doors to the Sacred. J Martos. SCM, 1981
On Becoming Christian H Bourgeois. St Paul, 1982
Credo: a Catholic Catechism. Geoffrey Chapman, 1983

Walk with me, Jesus,
Show me which road to take.

1 People of God

On the threshold of life

Lord, here I stand on the threshold of life
a new life...
It's like standing at the end of a long,
lonely dust road on a hot summer's day.
There's all road signs Lord, lots of them;
they're all offering me different things.
I don't know which road to take.
Must I choose the easiest one,
the smart highway,
or the muddy path,
the dust road, or...?

I know nothing of whom I'm going to meet
and the difficulties to be overcome.
But, Lord, do a friend a favour?
Help me to live fully,
no matter what!
And to be completely human.
Walk with me, Jesus.
Hold me by the hand.
Show me which road to take,
and help me get to the top.

Lord, make me truly human.

Key ideas

(*These three points show the important elements of doctrine, witness and prayer for each theme. They may be used as starting points or to summarise the theme at the end.*)

Christian doctrine: that you may understand that the Church as God's people is called to follow him as pilgrims on a journey of faith and love.

Christian living: that you may define and accept your responsibility as members of the Church.

Prayer and liturgy: that you may be guided into a deeper experience of prayer and Christian living.

Discussion points

(Questions to help you on your journey in faith)

1 Who or what brought you here today?
2 What do you hope to get out of these meetings?
3 The next few months may be a turning point or time of change in your life. What experience of turning points or changes in your life have you had already?
4 Who are the people who have most affected the way you see life?
5 Describe the kind of Church you belong to. What words and images suit your description? Are they personal or impersonal?
6 At Baptism you were called to belong to the Church. How do you experience this call today?
7 What are the main privileges and responsibilities of one who belongs to the People of God?
8 What aspects of Church life do you most closely identify with?

The word of God

God gives life to his people

The hand of the Lord was laid on me, and he carried me away by the spirit of the Lord and set me down in the middle of a valley, a valley full of bones. He made me walk up and down among them. There were vast quantities of these bones on the ground the whole length of the valley; and they were quite dried up. He said to me,
  'Son of man, can these bones live?'
  I said,
  'You know, Lord'.
  He said,
  'Prophesy over these bones. Say, "Dry bones, hear the word of the Lord. The Lord says this to these bones: I am now going to make the breath enter you, and you will live. I shall put sinews on you, I shall make flesh grow on you, I

shall cover you with skin and give you breath, and you will live: and you will learn that I am the Lord." '

I prophesied as I had been ordered. While I was prophesying, there was a noise, a sound of clattering; and the bones joined together. I looked, and saw that they were covered with sinews; flesh was growing on them and skin was covering them, but there was no breath in them. He said to me,

'Prophesy to the breath; prophesy, son of man. Say to the breath, "The Lord says this: Come from the four winds, breath; breathe on these dead; let them live!" '

I prophesied as he had ordered me, and the breath entered them; they came to life again and stood up on their feet, a great, an immense army. Then he said,

'Son of man, these bones are the whole House of Israel. They keep saying, "Our bones are dried up, our hope has gone; we are as good as dead". So prophesy. Say to them, "The Lord says this: I am now going to open your graves; I mean to raise you from your graves, my people, and lead you back to the soil of Israel. And you will know that I am the Lord, when I open your graves and raise you from your graves, my people. And I shall put my spirit in you, and you will live, and I shall resettle you on your own soil; and you will know that I, the Lord, have said and done this – it is the Lord who speaks." '

Ezechiel 37:1-14

The Spirit of God hovered over the waters at creation and brought life out of them. Then God breathed his Spirit into the dust and brought forth Adam.

When the people of God were in exile in Babylon and all hope seemed dead, the prophet Ezechiel reassured the people that God would bring life to the dry bones.

The Spirit given to us is a spirit of life, a spirit of freedom and a spirit of new purpose.

1 Where in your life and in the world do you want to see this new life of the Spirit?
2 In what ways do you and the world want to be set free?
3 In what ways could a new sense of purpose help you in your life as a disciple of Christ?

The life of the early Church

The first conversions

Hearing this, the people were cut to the heart and said to Peter and the apostles,

'What must we do, brothers?'

'You must repent,' Peter answered 'and every one of you must be baptised in the name of Jesus Christ for the forgiveness of your sins, and you will receive the gift of the Holy Spirit. The promise that was made is for you and your children, and for all those who are far away, for all those whom the Lord our God will call to himself.'

He spoke to them for a long time using many arguments, and he urged them,

'Save yourselves from this perverse generation.'

They were convinced by his arguments, and they accepted what he said and were baptised. That very day about three thousand were added to their number.

The early Christian community

These remained faithful to the teaching of the apostles, to the brotherhood, to the breaking of bread and to the prayers.

The many miracles and signs worked through the apostles made a deep impression on everyone.

The faithful all lived together and owned everything in common; they sold their goods and possessions and shared out the proceeds among themselves according to what each one needed.

They went as a body to the temple every day but met in their houses for the breaking of bread; they shared their food gladly and generously; they praised God and were looked up to by everyone. Day by day the Lord added to their community those destined to be saved.

Acts 2:37-47

1 'Repent'. What did this mean for the earliest disciples? What does it mean for you today?
2 Does this picture of the early Church help us to think more clearly about the Church of our own time?

The future Church

Then I saw a new heaven and a new earth; the first heaven and the first earth had disappeared now, and there was no longer any sea. I saw the holy city, and the new Jerusalem, coming down from God out of heaven, as beautiful as a bride all dressed for her husband. Then I heard a loud voice call from the throne,

'You see this city? Here God lives among men. He will make his home among them; they shall be his people, and he will be their God: his name is God-with-them. He will wipe away all tears from their eyes; there will be no more death, and no more mourning or sadness. The world of the past has gone.'

Then the One sitting on the throne spoke:

'Now I am making the whole of creation new' he said.

'Write this: that what I am saying is sure and will come true.'

And then he said,

'It is already done. I am the Alpha and the Omega, the Beginning and the End. I will give water from the well of life free to anybody who is thirsty; it is the rightful inheritance of the one who proves victorious; and I will be his God and he a son to me. But the legacy for cowards, for those who break their word, or worship obscenities, for murderers and fornicators, and for fortune-tellers, idolaters or any other sort of liars, is the second death in the burning lake of sulphur.'

Revelation 21:1-8

1 Which phrases describe the Church of the present and the Church of the future?
2 Is the promise 'Now I am making the whole of creation new' for the future only or for today as well?

The teaching of the Church

Images of the Church

In the Old Testament the revelation of the kingdom is often made under the forms of symbols. In similar fashion the inner nature of the Church is now made known to us in various images. Taken either from the life of the shepherd or from cultivation of the land, from the art of building or from family life and marriage, these images have their preparation in the books of the prophets.

Vatican II *Constitution on the Church* 6

The pilgrim Church

The Church, 'like a pilgrim in a foreign land, presses forward amid the persecutions of the world and the consolations of God,' announcing the cross and death of the Lord until he comes (compare 1 Cor. 11:26).

But by the power of the risen Lord she is given strength to overcome, in patience and in love, her sorrows and her difficulties, both those that are from within and those that are from without, so that she may reveal in the world, faithfully, however darkly, the mystery of her Lord until, in the consummation, it shall be manifested in full light.

Vatican II *Constitution on the Church* 8

1 Do you as a pilgrim feel yourself 'pressing forward' on your journey?
2 What are the sorrows and difficulties that you need to overcome?
3 How does the Church today reveal the mystery of the Lord?
4 Choose from the following the images that appeal to you the most. Discuss and think about them.

The Church is a sheepfold or a flock.
    John 10:1-15; Isaiah 40:11; Ezechiel 34:11-31

The Church is a tract of land to be cultivated, the field of God.
    1 Corinthians 3:9; Matthew 21:43; John 15:1-5

The Church is the edifice of God. The Lord is the cornerstone.
    1 Corinthians 3:9; Matthew 21:42; Psalm 118:22

The Church is the house of God.
    1 Timothy 3:15

The Church is a holy temple.
    1 Corinthians 3:16, 17

We are living stones.
    1 Peter 2:5

The Church is our mother.
    Galatians 4:26

The Church is the spouse of the Lamb.
    Revelation 19:7; Ephesians 5:29

Activities

1 Together, or in small groups, make a collage of the 'People of God'.
2 Make a poster advertising your Church, using one of the images you have discussed.
3 Put up some of your work in your Church.
4 Put together a statement of your beliefs about the Church, in the light of your discussion. Read it out at Mass or at a liturgical celebration.
5 Interview, after planning your questions, a committed Christian about his or her faith.
6 Discuss with your priest and members of the parish council the future of the Church in your area.
7 Find out something the Pope has said recently about the Church and share it with others in your group.

Prayer

Light a candle and pray together

Thanks be to you, my Lord Jesus Christ,
for all the benefits which you have given me,
for all the pains and insults
which you have borne for me:
O most merciful Redeemer, Friend and Brother,
may I know you more clearly,
love you more dearly,
follow you more nearly,
day by day.

St Richard of Chichester

Liturgy

After studying the word of God and the teaching of the Church and sharing some of the activities designed to deepen this study and relate it to life, the liturgy gives an opportunity to bind these different aspects together and share them with the wider community. These celebrations may be non-eucharistic and take place at any suitable time. Otherwise they may be used at a Sunday Mass. The necessary prayers are included below. The liturgy should always be adapted to suit local needs.

In the Mass the penitential rite and the bidding prayers (perhaps composed by the candidates themselves) should reflect that the candidates are entering a new stage of their journey in faith.

The candidates may be introduced and prayed for – perhaps by those who were confirmed in the previous year.

Candidates might read a statement of their beliefs about the Church and God's people. The Mass might end with a prayer of dedication and special blessing.

The feast of Christ the King celebrates Christ among his people. It is the end of the liturgical year and yet looks forward with vision and hope. This might be the occasion to draw together all those who have received a sacrament of initiation during the year and to pray for those who are to follow them.

A liturgy on the theme of the People of God

SONG

Be not afraid (*More Songs of the Spirit* 196)

INTRODUCTION

Priest We come together today to celebrate our unity as the people of God and the body of Christ. Today some young adults are beginning a new stage of their journey in faith as they think about preparing to receive the sacrament of Confirmation. We welcome their enthusiasm and their initiative and assure them of our prayer and support.

PENITENTIAL RITE

P Lord Jesus, high priest, you offered your life as the sacrifice to take away the sin of the world. Lord, have mercy.

All **Lord have mercy.**

P Christ Jesus, the prophet, by your words you guide your people on the way to the Father. Christ, have mercy.

A **Christ have mercy.**

P Lord Jesus, king and shepherd, you came to seek out and save those who were lost. Lord, have mercy.

A **Lord have mercy.**

PRAYER

P   Let us pray that the kingdom of Christ may live in our hearts
and come into our world:
Father all-powerful, God of love,
you have raised our Lord Jesus Christ
from death to life,
resplendent in glory as king of creation.
Open our hearts,
free all the world to rejoice in his peace,
to glory in his justice, to live in his love.
Bring all mankind together in Jesus Christ your son,
whose kingdom is with you and the Holy Spirit,
one God, for ever and ever.
Amen.

LITURGY OF THE WORD

READING

Ezechiel 37:1-14 The valley of dry bones. (*This reading
could be mimed or dramatised.*)
Psalm 103:1-2, 24, 27-30, 35 (*Grail Psalter*).

RESPONSE

A   **Send forth your spirit, O Lord,
and renew the face of the earth.**

GOSPEL

John 15:1-15

HOMILY

BIDDING PRAYERS

P   These candidates, our brothers and sisters, have already
travelled a long road. Let us thank God for his loving care
which has brought them to this day and ask that they may
continue to hasten toward complete fellowship in our
Christian way of life.

Reader That God our Father reveal his Christ to them more and
more with every passing day. Lord, hear us.

A   **Lord graciously hear us.**

R	That they undertake with generous hearts and souls whatever God may ask of them. Lord, hear us.
A	**Lord graciously hear us.**
R	That they have our sincere and unfailing support every step of the way. Lord, hear us.
A	**Lord graciously hear us.**
R	That our community offer them the persuasive witness of unity and generous love. Lord, hear us.
A	**Lord graciously hear us.**
R	That both they and we become ever more responsive to the needs of all. Lord, hear us.
A	**Lord graciously hear us.**
R	That they be found ready in due time to receive the new life of the Holy Spirit. Lord, hear us.
A	**Lord graciously hear us.**
P	Let us pray. God of all creation, keep your servants joyful in hope and faithful in your service. May the eternal joy you promise be the reward of all who spend their lives in good works. We ask this through Christ our Lord.
A	**Amen.**

LITURGY OF THE EUCHARIST

SONG

Moses, I know you're the man *(Celebration Hymnal* 197)

PRAYER

P	Lord, we offer you the sacrifice by which your Son reconciles mankind. May it bring unity and peace to the world. We ask this through Christ our Lord.
A	**Amen.**

PREFACE OF CHRIST THE KING

COMMUNION SONG

Bind us together (*Songs of the Spirit 69; Celebration Hymnal* 409)

PRAYER AFTER COMMUNION

P   Lord, you give us Christ, the King of all creation,
as food for everlasting life.
Help us to live by his gospel
and bring us to the joy of his kingdom,
where he lives and reigns for ever and ever.

A   **Amen.**

Candidates come forward and say together the following prayer:

Thanks be to you, my Lord Jesus Christ,
for all the benefits which you have given me,
for all the pains and insults
which you have borne for me:
O most merciful Redeemer, friend and brother,
may I know you more clearly,
love you more dearly,
follow you more nearly,
day by day.

P   The Lord be with you.
A   **And also with you.**
P   May the peace of God which is beyond all understanding keep your hearts and minds in the knowledge and love of God and of his Son, our Lord Jesus Christ.
A   **Amen.**

SONG

Sing to the mountains (*Songs of the Spirit 59*)

2 Advent

Come Lord Jesus

I need you to teach me day by day,
according to each day's opportunities and needs.

Give me, O my Lord, that purity of conscience
which alone can receive,
which alone can improve your inspiration.

My ears are dull,
so that I cannot hear your voice.
My eyes are dim,
so that I cannot see you
and the signs of your presence.

You alone can quicken my hearing,
and purge my sight,
and cleanse and renew my heart.
Teach me to sit at your feet
and to hear your Word.

John Henry Newman

A shoot springs from the stock of Jesse.

Key ideas

Christian doctrine: that you may understand the meaning of the Incarnation (literally the 'becoming flesh') and the continued presence of Christ in the world through the Holy Spirit.

Christian living: that you may appreciate that you receive God's love and mercy through the Incarnation of Jesus.

Prayer and liturgy: that you may prepare and celebrate a liturgy expressing the hope of God's people in the coming of Christ.

Discussion points

1 What do you look forward to most at Christmas?
2 Describe a happy experience related to Advent or Christmas.
3 What does it mean to you that 'we wait in joyful hope for the coming of our Saviour Jesus Christ'?
4 What do you mean when you call Jesus 'Saviour'?
5 'Prepare in the wilderness a way for the Lord'.
    Where is the wilderness today?
    What are you doing to prepare a way for the Lord?
6 'Thy kingdom come'.
    Where is the kingdom today?
    What can you do to make this prayer come true?

The word of God

The first coming of Christ

The Lord himself, therefore, will give you a sign.
    It is this: the maiden is with child and will soon give birth to a son whom she will call Immanuel.

Isaiah 7:14

1 How was this prophecy fulfilled for the Jews of Isaiah's time?
2 How is this promise fulfilled today for us?

The coming of the virtuous King

A shoot springs from the stock of Jesse,
a scion thrusts from his roots:
on him the spirit of the Lord rests,

a spirit of wisdom and insight,
a spirit of counsel and power,
a spirit of knowledge and of the fear of the Lord,
(The fear of the Lord is his breath.)
He does not judge by appearances,
he gives no verdict on hearsay,
but judges the wretched with integrity,
and with equity gives a verdict for the poor of the land.
His word is a rod that strikes the ruthless,
his sentences bring death to the wicked.
Integrity is the loincloth round his waist,
faithfulness the belt about his hips.
The wolf lives with the lamb,
the panther lies down with the kid,
calf and lion cub feed together
with a little boy to lead them.
The cow and the bear make friends,
their young lie down together.
The lion eats straw like the ox.
The infant plays over the cobra's hole;
into the viper's lair
the young child puts his hand.
They do no hurt, no harm,
on all my holy mountain,
for the country is filled with the knowledge of the Lord
as the waters swell the sea.

Isaiah 11:1-9

1 Notice the equipment of the king (lines 3 to 5).
2 Notice how he exercises his authority (lines 8 to 15).
3 Notice the peace that comes with his reign (16 to end).
4 Notice that from this passage we derive the traditional seven gifts of the Holy Spirit.

Peter predicts the second coming of Christ

My friends, this is my second letter to you and in both of them I have tried to awaken a true understanding in you by giving you a reminder recalling to you what was said in the past by the holy prophets and the commandments of the Lord and saviour which you were given by the apostles.

Recall briefly the message of the holy prophets and the commandments of our Lord which were given by the apostles.

> We must be careful to remember that during the last days there are bound to be people who will be scornful, the kind who always please themselves what they do, and they will make fun of the promise and ask
>
> 'Well, where is this coming? Everything goes on as it has since the Fathers died, as it has since it began at the creation'.
>
> They are choosing to forget that there were heavens at the beginning, and that the earth was formed by the word of God out of water and between the waters, so that the world of that time was destroyed by being flooded by water. But by the same word, the present sky and earth are destined for fire, and are only being reserved until Judgement day so that all sinners may be destroyed.

1 What is the promise to which Peter refers?
2 Why did scornful people make fun of it?

> But there is one thing, my friends, that you must never forget: that with the Lord, 'a day' can mean a thousand years, and a thousand years is like a day.
>
> The Lord is not being slow to carry out his promises, as anybody else might be called slow; but he is being patient with you all, wanting nobody to be lost and everybody to be brought to change his ways.
>
> The Day of the Lord will come like a thief, and then with a roar the sky will vanish, the elements will catch fire and fall apart, the earth and all that it contains will be burnt up.

What is the 'day' to which Peter refers?

> Since everything is coming to an end like this, you should be living holy and saintly lives while you wait and long for the Day of God to come, when the sky will dissolve in flames and the elements melt in the heat. What we are waiting for is what he promised: the new heavens and new earth, the place where righteousness will be at home.
>
> So then, my friends, while you are waiting, do your best to live lives without spot or stain so that he will find you at peace. Think of our Lord's patience as your opportunity to be saved.

> Our brother Paul, who is so dear to us, told you this when he wrote to you with the wisdom that is his special gift. He always writes like this when he deals with this sort of subject, and this makes some points in his letter hard to understand; these are the points that uneducated and unbalanced people distort, in the same way as they distort the rest of scripture – a fatal thing for them to do.

What are the points which 'uneducated and unbalanced people distort'?

> You have been warned about this, my friends; be careful not to get carried away by the errors of unprincipled people, from the firm ground that you are standing on. Instead, go on growing in the grace and in the knowledge of our Lord and saviour Jesus Christ. To him be glory, in time and in eternity. Amen.

> 2 Peter 3:1-18

What is the 'firm ground' on which we stand?

The teaching of the Church

Advent

'We wait in joyful hope for the coming of our Lord and Saviour, Jesus Christ.'

Advent means coming or arrival. During Advent we relive the experience of those who waited for the birth of the messiah – the Christ. We do not simply remember, or even re-enact their waiting. We too are experiencing a time of longing for the coming of our Saviour. We experience this longing, as a Church, through the liturgy of Advent. Every event we recall in the liturgy brings to mind the ways in the past in which God came to meet his people. We recall in the words of scripture and the celebration of the eucharist how God comes to meet us today.

The season of Advent is a time of conversion and renewal. We experience the darkness in fasting and penance as we reflect on our need for God. We reflect on how God comes to us in our darkness. His light in our lives is one of the themes of the prophets, especially of Isaiah. Isaiah was very conscious of the love of God which would be shown in the sending of his anointed – the messiah. 'Have courage, fear not, behold your God'.

John the Baptist, too, is a key figure in the Advent liturgy. As the crowds stood at the banks of the Jordan, listening with intensity and interest, so do we stand, listening to the promises and the warnings of the one who urges us too to prepare a way for the Lord in today's desert and wilderness.

Mary appears in the liturgy as one who took to heart the message of God about the advent of his Son, and took to herself, through the power of the Holy Spirit, the Son of God to be born into our world, a man like us in all things but sin. Mary expresses, in the readings, both her faith in God's plan, and her joy in the advent of the Saviour.

Isaiah, John the Baptist and Mary in their different ways herald the coming of Christ with desolation and expectation, nostalgia and joy. Advent for us is a time of mixed feelings, a time of sorrow but of hope. We celebrate the first coming of Christ in the Incarnation; we anticipate the second coming of Christ for the end of the world and for judgement. In between these comings, we celebrate the presence of Christ in the Spirit.

Those who are to be confirmed remember the coming of the Spirit at their Baptism. Through this sacrament they became part of God's faithful people. Now they anticipate in a special way the outpouring of the Holy Spirit in their own personal Pentecost which will be celebrated sacramentally at their Confirmation.

Advent is celebrated by a number of customs. One important symbol is that of lighting the candles of the Advent wreath which reminds us of the coming of Jesus Christ, our light.

Activities

1 Look at and discuss the kind of Christmas cards people send and the messages they convey.
2 Look at various Advent customs. Make an Advent wreath, an Advent calendar or a Jesse tree. Take them home and share them with your family. Take them to church for Sunday Mass.
3 Role play the way in which various people look forward to Christmas, e.g. a shopkeeper, a tramp, a bus driver, a priest, a nurse, a child, etc.
4 Make a poster illustrating the Isaiah text 'He sent me to bring good news...' (Isaiah 61:1 and following), showing who today are the blind, the captives, those in sorrow, etc., and how they are to be set free.

Prayer

Light a candle and conclude with the prayer of St Patrick:

I bind unto myself today
the power of God to hold and lead:
his eye to watch, his might to say,
his ear to hearken to my need;
the wisdom of my God to teach,
his hand to guide, his shield to ward;
the Word of God to give me speech,
his heavenly host to be my guard.

Christ be with me, Christ within me,
Christ behind me, Christ before me,
Christ beside me, Christ to win me,
Christ to comfort and restore me.
Christ beneath me, Christ above me,
Christ in quiet, Christ in danger,
Christ in hearts of all that love me,
Christ in mouth of friend and stranger.

Liturgy

Prepare an Advent service for your group or for your family, friends
and parishioners, especially the elderly. The service might contain the
following:

Introduction: preparing the way of the Lord; expression of sorrow and conversion; some explanation of the symbols of Advent, e.g. light, wreath.

Penitential prayers.

Gospel reading.

Bidding prayers.

Action, mime or drama, involving gold, incense, myrrh with lights, Advent wreath, toys or gifts for the poor.

Some experience of reconciliation: e.g. sign of peace or sacramental confession.

Alternatively you could use the liturgy that follows.

An Advent liturgy

SONG

Here I am, Lord (Dan Schutte, SJ)

GREETING

Priest   May the peace and love of Christ come into your hearts, now and always.

All   **Amen.**

INTRODUCTION

P   All life is a process of becoming. We have never completely arrived, but are always on the move and waiting. We wait for tomorrow to come – sometimes eagerly, sometimes fearfully. Advent is a time of cheerful waiting. We cannot avoid fear and suffering in our lives, but this season is a reminder to us that we need not be slaves to fear. The message of Advent is that if we learn to follow Christ we will become free. We are waiting for him to be born in our hearts.

The Advent wreath is brought in.

The Advent wreath is a sign of the passage of time, and of the gradual approach of God to us in our lives. As we listen to each of these five short Readings we can think about the welcome we have given to God in our lives.

FIRST READING

Light the first candle

Reader   God shows himself to us in the whole of creation. Genesis
         1:1-5
R   For our failure to recognise you in the glory of your world;
         Lord, have mercy.
A   **Christ have mercy.**

SECOND READING

Light the second candle

R   God shows himself to us in man and woman. Genesis
         1:26-28
R   For our failure to know you in our fellow men; Lord, have
         mercy.
A   **Christ have mercy.**

THIRD READING

Light the third candle

R   God tells us that we are his family. Ezechiel 36:25-28
R   For our failure to live up to our Baptism;
         Lord, have mercy.
A   **Christ have mercy.**

FOURTH READING

Light the fourth candle

R   God tells us that through his prophet that he will always be
         with us. Isaiah 7:14
R   For our failure to find you in our daily lives;
         Lord, have mercy.
A   **Christ have mercy.**

PRAYER

P   Let us pray.
         Lord God, creator of the universe,
         you have shown us yourself in all you have done,
         and have promised to be with us always.
         Help us to be willing and waiting to receive you
         through Jesus Christ our Lord.
A   **Amen.**

GOSPEL READING

P   God came to Mary, to invite her to accept his presence. Luke 1:26-36

BIDDING PRAYERS

P   Let us pray for a clear vision of God and for the readiness to respond faithfully to this vision. Lord hear us.

A   **Lord graciously hear us.**

P   We pray, Lord, for all those in authority, that they may see you in those they lead, and may learn to be true servants. Lord hear us.

A   **Lord graciously hear us.**

P   We pray, Lord, for those searching for a faith to live by that they may open their hearts to your presence in the world. Lord hear us.

A   **Lord graciously hear us.**

P   We pray, Lord, for those who spend their time waiting for an answer, that they may learn how to hear you. Lord hear us.

A   **Lord graciously hear us.**

P   We pray, Lord, for those whose lives are full of bitterness and despondency, that in this season Christ may become a light to them. Lord hear us.

A   **Lord graciously hear us.**

OFFERTORY PROCESSION AND SONG

PRAYER OVER THE GIFTS

P   Father, we bring you this food and drink which are the signs of your caring presence. We pray that as they become the true presence of your Son we may become closer to you, and to each other. We make our prayer through Christ our Lord.

A   **Amen.**

COMMUNION SONG

PRAYER AFTER COMMUNION

P   Lord God, from the beginning of time you have invited men to share your love. May this communion help us always to be in communion with you and to be ready for your coming. We make our prayer through Jesus Christ who is God with us.

A   **Amen.**

SONG

Our God reigns (*More Songs of the Spirit* 134)

A liturgy of enrolment

After two months of discussion, prayer and reflection, the candidates are invited to enrol in a programme of preparation to receive the sacrament of Confirmation. The bishop (or dean or parish priest) presides at the service and receives the names of the candidates.

During the next stage of the catechumenate the candidates will experience a more formal presentation of the faith, a greater intensity of prayer and an encouragement to perform good works in the service of God and neighbour. At the end of this stage, the candidates may make a formal request to receive the sacrament.

SONG

INTRODUCTION

Dean   We have come together today as God's family to celebrate his
or   love and to reflect on his invitation to follow him and serve
priest him in love. Some of you are considering the call to receive
         the fullness of the gift of his Spirit in the sacrament of
         Confirmation. Let us listen to the word of God and reflect on
         the kind of life to which we are being invited.

READING

Ephesians 3:14 – 4:6

SONG

HOMILY

PRESENTATION OF THE CANDIDATES

Dean   My Lord, we offer to you the young people of (N.) deanery
         [or parish] who wish to enter into a time of preparation to
         receive the sacrament of Confirmation.

THE SCRUTINY

Bishop You are here today in order to declare before me, your
         bishop, and before members of your parish communities,
         your intention to share in the life of the Holy Spirit through

the sacrament of Confirmation. I now ask you:

Are you prepared to commit yourself to a time of prayer and study so that you may understand more clearly the meaning of the sacrament you wish to receive?

Candi- **I am, with the help of the Holy Spirit.**
dates

B   Are you prepared to offer yourself, your time and your faith to serve your parish communities in whatever way you can?

C   **I am, with the help of the Holy Spirit.**

B   Are you prepared to accept the call to witness to the presence of Christ among his people?

C   **I am, with the help of the Holy Spirit.**

B   Are you prepared to open your heart and mind so that the Holy Spirit may live within you?

C   **I am, with the help of the Holy Spirit.**

The Bishop now addresses the whole congregation.

B   Do you understand that the gifts of the Spirit are given to us for the good of the whole Church?

All   **We do.**

B   Do you therefore accept these members of your parishes as candidates for the sacrament of Confirmation?

A   **We do.**

B   Do you promise to share in their preparation for this sacrament by your prayers, your encouragement and your example?

A   **We do.**

The Bishop now addresses the candidates.

B   May the faith and zeal you now have be with you and grow within you throughout your lives. In the name of the Church in this diocese, and in the name of your parish communities, I accept you as worthy candidates for the sacrament of Confirmation.

A   **Thanks be to God.**

The candidates now come forward to present their enrolment cards to the Bishop. A song may be sung.

BIDDING PRAYERS

B   Guided by the Holy Spirit, let us now come in prayer before our heavenly Father asking for those things which will enable us to live more fully the life of Christ.

Reader   We pray for the parish communities of this deanery. Father, may the witness and example of Christian life that we present to others be an inspiration to them and the source of faith and hope in their lives. Lord, hear us.

A   **Lord graciously hear us.**

R   We pray for all those in our diocese who are soon to receive the sacrament of Confirmation. Father, we thank you for the faith which already fills the lives of these people. During their time of prayer and preparation may their hearts and minds be open and ready to accept the gifts of your Spirit. Lord, hear us.

A   **Lord graciously hear us.**

R   We pray for the priests, teachers and catechists who are involved in the programme of preparation.

Father, be with those who have the ministry of teaching in your Church. Your Spirit is the Spirit of truth. Fill their minds and hearts with knowledge and understanding of our faith and guide them so that their word and example may lead us closer to you. Lord, hear us.

A   **Lord graciously hear us.**

R   We pray for those who seek faith, for those who search for a meaning and value in life.

Father, as we rejoice in our faith we remember those who lack the consolation and hope which comes from knowing you and the Good News of our salvation. Come into the lives of all who seek you with sincerity of heart. Lord, hear us.

A   **Lord graciously hear us.**

R   We now pray for our own special needs, and for the needs of those around us today.

B   Let us now pray for ourselves, our parishes, this deanery and our diocese.

A   **Lord Jesus Christ,**
Son of the living God,
teach us to walk in your way more trustfully,
to accept your truth more faithfully,
and to share your life more lovingly.
By the power of the Holy Spirit
help us to live more generously
as your disciples
so that we may all come
as one family
to the kingdom of the Father

	where you live and reign
	for ever and ever. Amen.
B	The Lord be with you.
A	**And also with you.**
Deac-	
on	Bow your heads for God's blessing.
B	Go forth into the world in peace;
	be of good courage;
	hold fast to that which is good;
	render no one evil for evil;
	strengthen the faint-hearted;
	support the weak;
	help the afflicted;
	honour all people;
	love and serve the Lord,
	rejoicing in the power of the Holy Spirit.
	And may the blessing of almighty God,
	the Father, the Son and the Holy Spirit
	be with you now and evermore.
A	**Amen.**

SONG

3 Baptism

Make us worthy, Lord,
to serve our fellow men
throughout the world
who live and die
in poverty and hunger.

Give them through our hands
this day their daily bread,
and by our understanding love,
give peace and joy.

Mother Teresa of Calcutta

Key ideas

Christian doctrine: that you may understand that Baptism is the sacrament by which new members enter into the Christian community.

Christian living: that you may value this sacrament of initiation as a reflection of the love and concern of Jesus.

Prayer and liturgy: that you may experience the liturgy of Baptism as a symbolic celebration of our life in Christ.

Discussion points

1 How do we express in our lives the idea that we are 'children of God' and 'brothers and sisters in Christ'?
2 Baptism is the sacrament of our salvation. What are we 'saved from' and 'saved for' in this sacrament?
3 How do the various symbols used in the rite of Baptism help to unfold the meaning of this sacrament?
4 What links do you find between the rite of Baptism and the celebration of the Easter mystery, and between the rite of Confirmation and the celebration of the event of Pentecost?

Parents may also like to discuss the following:

5 What were the reasons for having your child baptised?
6 Where were your hopes and fears for your child at that time?
7 What are your hopes and fears for your child today?

The word of God

John baptises Jesus

Then Jesus appeared: he came from Galilee to the Jordan to
be baptised by John. John tried to dissuade him.
'It is I who need baptism from you' he said
'and yet you come to me!'
But Jesus replied,
'Leave it like this for the time being; it is fitting that we
should, in this way, do all that righteousness demands'.
At this, John gave in to him.
As soon as Jesus was baptised he came up from the water,
and suddenly the heavens opened and he saw the Spirit of
God descending like a dove and coming down on him. And a
voice spoke from heaven,
'This is my Son, the Beloved; my favour rests on him'.
Matthew 3:13-17

Jesus was baptised to receive the Spirit for his mission of teaching
and healing.
In his Baptism Jesus is revealed as the Son of God and the (suffering)
servant.

1 When people are baptised, how does their relationship with God
   and their neighbour change?
2 In what way do Christians carry on the special mission of Jesus
   today?

The teaching of Jesus

Jesus' conversation with Nicodemus

There was one of the Pharisees called Nicodemus, a leading
Jew, who came to Jesus by night and said,
'Rabbi, we know that you are a teacher who comes from

God; for no one could perform the signs that you do unless
God were with him'.
Jesus answered:

'I tell you most solemnly,
unless a man is born from above,
he cannot see the kingdom of God'.

Nicodemus said,
'How can a grown man be born? Can he go back into his
mother's womb and be born again?'
Jesus replied:

'I tell you most solemnly,
unless a man is born through water and the Spirit,
he cannot enter the kingdom of God:
what is born of the flesh is flesh;
what is born of the Spirit is spirit.
Do not be surprised when I say:
You must be born from above.
The wind blows wherever it pleases;
you hear its sound,
but you cannot tell where it comes from or where it is going.
That is how it is with all who are born of the Spirit.'

John 3:1-8

1 This passage teaches that Baptism is for re-birth. The phrases 'from
  above' and 'born again' show that this is a spiritual transformation.
  What does Jesus mean by 'entering the kingdom of God'?
2 The dialogue between Nicodemus and Jesus which leads to his
  gradual understanding of the meaning of Jesus' teaching mirrors
  perhaps our own growth in understanding the meaning of our
  Baptism. Has your understanding of your own Baptism grown
  deeper through your discussion of this passage?

The teaching of St Paul

The meaning of our Baptism

Does it follow that we should remain in sin so as to let grace
have greater scope?

   Of course not. We are dead to sin, so how can we continue
to live in it?

You have been taught that when we were baptised in Christ Jesus we were baptised in his death; in other words, when we were baptised we went into the tomb with him and joined him in death, so that as Christ was raised from the dead by the Father's glory, we too might live a new life. If in union with Christ we have imitated his death, we shall also imitate him in his resurrection.

We must realise that our former selves have been crucified with him to destroy this sinful body and to free us from the slavery of sin. When a man dies, of course, he has finished with sin.

But we believe that having died with Christ we shall return to life with him: Christ, as we know, having been raised from the dead will never die again. Death has no power over him any more. When he died, he died, once for all, to sin, so his life now is life with God; and in that way, you too must consider yourselves to be dead to sin but alive for God in Christ Jesus.

Romans 6:1-11

1 Discuss how Paul brings out the spiritual meaning of Baptism through the images of dying and rising.
2 How can we show that we are 'dead to sin' and 'alive for God'?

The teaching of the Church

The prayers of the Liturgy of Baptism show how we become disciples of Christ. They point the way to Confirmation by referring to the baptised person as living like Christ, the priest, the prophet and the king. Read these extracts carefully.

From the rite of Baptism for children

To fulfil the true meaning of the sacrament (baptism), children must later be formed in the faith in which they have been baptised. The foundation of this formation will be the sacrament itself, which they have already received.

Christian formation, which is their due, seeks to lead them gradually to learn God's plan in Christ, so that they may ultimately accept for themselves the faith in which they have been baptised (Rite no.3).

The celebrant speaks to the parents in these or similar words:

You have asked to have your children baptised. In doing so you are accepting the responsibility of training them in the practice of the faith. It will be your duty to bring them up to keep God's commandments as Christ taught us, by loving God and our neighbour. Do you clearly understand what you are undertaking?

Parents: **We do.** (Rite no.39)

The priest speaks these words directly to the children as he anoints each infant with chrism:

God the Father of our Lord Jesus Christ has freed you from sin, given you a new birth by water and the Holy Spirit, and welcomed you into his holy people. He now anoints you with the chrism of salvation. As Christ was anointed Priest, Prophet, and King, so may you live always as members of his body, sharing everlasting life.

All: **Amen.** (Rite no.61)

Standing before the Easter candle the celebrant says:

Receive the light of Christ.

Someone from each family then lights the child's candle from the Easter candle. The celebrant says:

Parents and godparents, this light is entrusted to you to be kept burning brightly. These children of yours have been enlightened by Christ. They are to walk always as children of the light. May they keep the flame of faith alive in their hearts. (Rite no.63)

After the baptism the priest addresses all who are present:

Dearly beloved, these children have been reborn in baptism. They are now called children of God, for so indeed they are. In confirmation they will receive the fullness of God's Spirit. In holy communion they will share the banquet of Christ's sacrifice, calling God their Father in the midst of the Church. In their name, in the Spirit of our common sonship, let us pray together in the words our Lord has given us:

All present join the celebrant in singing or saying the Our Father. (Rite no.67)

1 Who are the people who have had the greatest influence on the way you see your faith?
2 How has an understanding of God's plan been unfolded in your life?
3 In Baptism, we are anointed to live as members of his body. What are the most important ways we do this?
4 After Baptism, candidates are to walk as children of the light. What does this mean in practical terms?

Pope John Paul II, Westminster 1982

'In Baptism we are drawn into the community of faith. We become part of the pilgrim people of God, which, in all times and in all places, goes forward in hope towards the fulfilment of the "promise" '.

1 If you were invited to act as sponsor for an adult being baptised today, how would you help him or her to appreciate what is meant by a community of faith?

'Baptism creates a sacramental body of unity linking all who have been reborn by means of it.
'But Baptism, of itself, is only a beginning, a point of departure for it is wholly directed towards the fulness of life in Christ.'

2 Pause briefly to consider who, in your journey, has helped you most so far in your life.
3 In what ways could people in your parish be encouraged to be aware of their responsibility to be active members of the community of faith.

'We the baptised have work to do together as brothers and sisters in Christ. The world is in need of Jesus Christ and his gospel – the Good news.'

4 We are all aware of the priest's role in spreading the Good News. What responsibility has the layperson?
5 What opportunities do you have to spread the Good News?

We speak of Baptism as 'the foundation of unity that all Christians have in Christ' and we hear the Pope say that 'we feel ashamed that we have not all been capable of maintaining full unity of faith and charity that Christ willed for his Church'.

6 How do we fulfil our role in seeking to perfect this unity, especially in regard to baptised Christians who owe allegiance to other churches?

Activities

1 Fill in a record of your journey in faith (see page 104).
2 Ask about the events surrounding your own Baptism.
3 Role play the Rite of Baptism, taking different parts. Write or give a commentary where appropriate.
4 Write your own version of the baptismal promises – the rejection of sin and the act of faith – to express in your own words the beliefs you proclaim and the evils you reject.
5 Interview a couple who have recently had a baby about the Baptism of their child.

Prayer

Light a candle and pray together.

Lord Jesus,
through the sacrament of Baptism
you offer the gift of divine life
to those who trust in you.

Through Baptism
you call your followers
to spread the good news of God's love
which can set us free.

Open our hearts to your gift of life.
Help us to be faithful
to the mission you have given us.

Strengthen us
to keep your commandments
by loving you and our neighbour.
Keep us faithful to your teaching.
Never let us be parted from you.

Peter Humfrey

Liturgy

1 Join a family group as they prepare for the Baptism of their child.
2 Join in the celebration of a Baptism, taking part in the prayers and responses.
3 Compose a Penitential Rite and Bidding prayers for a Sunday Mass, which express some of the ideas you have discussed.
4 Organise a prayer service using the paschal candle and blessed water. Choose readings, poems and prayers to express your ideas about Baptism. Or use the following:

A liturgy on the theme of Baptism

SONG

Come to the water (*More Songs of the Spirit* 182)

BLESSING OF THE WATER

Candidates come forward to the altar.

Priest   Dear friends,
this water will be used
to remind us of our Baptism.
Let us ask God to bless it
and to keep us faithful
to the Spirit he has given us.

God our Father,
your gift of water
brings life and freshness on the earth;
it washes away our sins
and brings us eternal life.
We ask you now
to bless this water
and give us your protection on this day
which you have made your own.
Renew the living spring of your life within us
and protect us in Spirit and body,
that we may be free from sin
and come into your presence
to receive your gift of salvation.
We ask this through Christ our Lord.

A   **Amen.**

*The candidates come in turn to the water, dip in their hand and make
the sign of the cross. The celebrant then sprinkles the congregation
with the water. A song may be sung.*

P   May almighty God cleanse us of our sins, and through the
      Eucharist we celebrate make us worthy to sit at his table in
      his heavenly kingdom.
A   **Amen.**

LITURGY OF THE WORD

READING

Romans 6:3-11
Psalms 41:2-3; 42:3-4

RESPONSE

A   **My soul is thirsting for God, the God of my life.**

GOSPEL

P   Those who wish to make the Lord's Prayer part of their life
      please come forward.
Candidates come forward.
P   This is how the Lord taught his disciples to pray.
      Matthew 6:9-13

HOMILY

*The celebrant explains the meaning and importance of the Lord's
Prayer.*

BIDDING PRAYERS

P   Let us pray for the candidates and for all God's people.
Reader That these candidates for Confirmation may find joy in daily
        prayer, let us pray. Lord hear us.
A   **Lord graciously hear us.**
R   That by praying to you often they may live in ever closer
        union with you, let us pray. Lord hear us.
A   **Lord graciously hear us.**
R   That they may joyfully read your word and ponder it in their
        hearts, let us pray. Lord hear us.
A   **Lord graciously hear us.**

R   That they may turn their daily work into an offering pleasing to you, let us pray. Lord hear us.
A   **Lord graciously hear us.**
R   That they may share with others the joy they have derived from their faith, let us pray. Lord hear us.
A   **Lord graciously hear us.**
P   Lord, you call these chosen ones to the glory of new birth in the Spirit. Help them to grow in wisdom and love as they prepare to profess their faith in you. We ask this through Christ our Lord.
A   **Amen.**

LITURGY OF THE EUCHARIST

SONG

Freely, freely (*Songs of the Spirit* 12)

PRAYER OVER THE GIFTS

P   Lord, you welcome us to your table
where bread and wine are prepared for us.
May we who celebrate this eucharistic feast
be counted as fellow-citizens of the saints
and members of your household.
We ask this through Christ our Lord.
A   **Amen.**

COMMUNION SONG

Song for a young prophet (*Songs of the Spirit* 20)

PRAYER AFTER COMMUNION

P   Lord, in this Eucharist we proclaim the death and resurrection of your Son. May the power of this sacrament give us courage to proclaim it also in our lives. We ask this through Christ our Lord.
A   **Amen.**

One or all of the candidates reads the following prayer.

R   Lord Jesus, through the sacrament of Baptism you offer the gift of divine life to those who trust in you.

Through Baptism you call your followers to spread the good news of God's love which can set us free.

Open our hearts to your gift of life. Help us to be faithful to the mission you have given us.

Strengthen us to keep your commandments by loving you and our neighbour.

Keep us faithful to your teaching. Never let us be parted from you.

BLESSING

SONG

Colours of Day (*Celebration Hymnal* 45)

Open our hearts to your gift of life.

4 Reconciliation

Father,
We know that you are love
and that by living in love
we live in you.

We know that you are light
and that by walking in light
we walk with you.

We recognise that we do not
always respond in love;
that we sometimes walk
in darkness.

We come together to ask your help,
and to help and support one another.
We are here to seek your healing,
and to heal one another.

Make us one with you and all people.
Give us your Spirit of peace and joy.

Peter Humfrey

Key ideas

Christian doctrine: that you may understand more fully that the mission of Jesus was to reconcile people to one another and to the Father through his teaching, his healing and his death on the cross.

Christian living: that you may be reconciled to God and fulfil a mission of sharing this reconciliation with others.

Prayer and liturgy: that you may prepare for a fruitful celebration of sacramental reconciliation in your group or community.

Discussion points

1 Give examples of the ways in which the goodness and love of

people have built up (a) the created world, (b) people in the world, and (c) your own life.

2 How important is it to hear the word of God and respond to it? What happens when people fail to hear God's word or choose to ignore it?

3 Do you think you are in any way personally responsible for the good there is in the world? For the evil?

4 Is 'conversion' a change of mind or a change of heart?

5 Where in your life have you forgiven others or been forgiven? How did you show forgiveness or have it shown to you?

6 If we have really been forgiven and reconciled, should it show?

7 Look up the three rites of Reconciliation in the Church and see how they can help us to be reconciled to God and to each other.

The word of God

Jesus cures a paralytic

When Jesus returned to Capernaum some time later, word went round that he was back; and so many people collected that there was no room left, even in front of the door.

He was preaching the word to them when some people came bringing him a paralytic carried by four men, but as the crowd made it impossible to get the man to him, they stripped the roof over the place where Jesus was; and when they had made an opening, they lowered the stretcher on which the paralytic lay.

Seeing their faith, Jesus said to the paralytic,

'My child, your sins are forgiven'.

Now some scribes were sitting there, and they thought to themselves,

'How can this man talk like that? He is blaspheming. Who can forgive sins but God?'

Jesus, inwardly aware that this was what they were thinking, said to them,

'Why do you have these thoughts in your hearts? Which of these is easier: to say to the paralytic, "Your sins are forgiven" or to say, "Get up, pick up your stretcher and walk"? But to prove to you that the Son of Man has authority on earth to forgive sins,' – he said to the paralytic –

'I order you: get up, pick up your stretcher, and go off home.'

And the man got up, picked up his stretcher at once and walked out in front of everyone, so that they were all astounded and praised God saying,

'We have never seen anything like this'.

Mark 2:1-12

1 What kind of person did the people in the story take Jesus to be?
2 What did Jesus reveal about his power to see a man's heart?
3 Why did Jesus forgive the man's sins before he healed his paralysis?
4 Does the reaction of the bystanders reveal what kind of authority Jesus had?
5 Would it be fair to say that the scribes were the real sinners? Who did they think Jesus was?
6 What part does faith play in this story?

Jesus meets Zacchaeus

Jesus entered Jericho and was going through the town when a man whose name was Zacchaeus made his appearance; he was one of the senior tax collectors and a wealthy man. He was anxious to see what kind of man Jesus was, but he was too short and could not see him for the crowd; so he ran ahead and climbed a sycamore tree to catch a glimpse of Jesus who was to pass that way. When Jesus reached the spot he looked up and spoke to him:

'Zacchaeus, come down. Hurry, because I must stay at your house today.'

And he hurried down and welcomed him joyfully. They all complained when they saw what was happening.

'He has gone to stay at a sinner's house' they said.

But Zacchaeus stood his ground and said to the Lord,

'Look, sir, I am going to give half my property to the poor, and if I have cheated anybody I will pay him back four times the amount'.

And Jesus said to him,

'Today salvation has come to this house, because this man too is a son of Abraham; for the Son of Man has come to seek out and save what was lost'.

Luke 19:1-10

1 Describe the kind of person Zacchaeus was (wealthy, villain, profiteer, extortioner, outcast, 'unclean'?).

2 Who makes the first move?
3 Describe some of the changes that would have occurred as a result of Zacchaeus meeting Jesus.
4 Who was helped by Zacchaeus' conversion?
5 What is the significance of the word 'Today'?

The teaching of the Church
From the Rite of Penance

The mystery of reconciliation in the history of salvation

1   The Father has shown forth his mercy by reconciling the world to himself in Christ, making peace through the blood of his cross, both as to the things that are on earth and the things that are in heaven.

When the Son of God became man, he lived among men so as to free them from the slavery of sin and call them out of darkness into his marvellous light. For this reason he began his work on earth by preaching penitence with the words: 'Repent, and believe the good news' (Mark 1:15).

Jesus, however, not only exhorted men to repent so as to leave their sinful ways and turn to God with all their hearts. He himself welcomed sinners and reconciled them to God. Moreover, he healed the sick, as a sign that he was able to forgive sin, and finally died for our sins and rose again for our justification.

On the night that he was betrayed, at the beginning of his redeeming Passion, he instituted the sacrifice of the new covenant in his blood for the remission of sins, and after his Resurrection he sent his Holy Spirit on the apostles, giving them the power of binding and loosing men's sins. Theirs was to be the task of preaching repentance and forgiveness of sins to all nations.

Repentance in the life and liturgy of the Church

4   The people of God continue this work of repentance in many different ways. They share the sufferings of Christ through patient endurance, they do works of mercy and charity, striving always more and more to live according to Christ's gospel, and so they become a sign to their fellow men of all that conversion to God implies.

This is what the church expresses and celebrates in her liturgy when the faithful confess themselves to be sinners, and pray God's forgiveness for themselves and for others. This takes place

in penitential services,
in the proclamation of God's word,
in prayer,
and in the penitential rite of the mass.

The function of the community in celebrating Penance

5   The whole church, as a priestly people, has its part to play in the work of reconciliation entrusted to it, and this it does in several ways. Not only does it call sinners to repentance by preaching the word of God, but it also intercedes for them and cares for them as a mother, so that they may acknowledge and confess their sins, and so receive mercy from God, who alone can forgive sin. Moreover, the church is the instrument by which the sinner is converted and absolved through the ministry given by Christ to his apostles and to their successors.

In the passages above, notice the following points:

1   Reconciliation is a mystery. It is part of the history of salvation.
2   Jesus lived among the people and called them from sin and darkness to freedom and light.
3   Jesus walked with and ate with sinners.
4   The blood of the cross of Jesus is the climax and fulfilment of God's plan of salvation.
5   Jesus gave the power of the Holy Spirit to his apostles for the forgiveness of sins.
6   The Church continues and celebrates the reconciling work of Jesus.

Sacramental Confession

1   How do you feel about confession?
2   Do you think all sin can be put down to selfishness?
3   Do you find your sense of what is sinful changes as you get older?
4   What is the best part of sacramental confession for you?

a sense of God's forgiveness
a sense of being one with the Church again
a chance to talk in confidence

the opportunity to discuss problems
getting rid of guilt
feeling better afterwards
making a fresh start.

5 Do you find taking part in a community service of reconciliation more or less helpful than individual confession?

Activities

1 Find newspaper headlines or articles which show good news and bad news in the world, and in your local community.
   Show how God's message of love and healing could be conveyed in these situations.
   Illustrate this by making your own newspage.
2 Think about the choices you make in daily life. Act out some situations where there are moral choices to be made, e.g. where lying, cheating, shoplifting or other events have caused a breakdown in good relationships.
   Discuss the alternative choices which would lead to a different outcome.
3 Look at the Ten Commandments of the Old Testament (Exodus 20:1-17) and the Two Commandments of the New Testament (Luke 10:25-28). How could a knowledge and understanding of these help you in times of decision?
4 List and discuss the signs of forgiveness and reconciliation you see in everyday life. How does the church use signs of forgiveness, e.g. ashes, water, lighted candles, the laying on of hands, etc?

Prayer

In the Sermon on the Mount (Matthew, chapters 5 and 6) the old way of the Law is replaced by the new way of Christ in social and religious matters.
1 Social action
   Not only is killing forbidden but even anger is to be replaced by reconciliation and 'coming to terms'. (5:21-24)

   Swearing oaths is to be replaced by simple speech. (5:33-37)

   Hatred is to be replaced by love and prayer. (5:43-48)
2 Religious action
   Charitable work is not to be trumpeted but done in secret. (6:1-4)

Prayer is not to be hypocritical but in the heart; pray not as the pagans do but as Jesus taught. (6:5-13)

Fasting is not to be done to impress others but to be secret and known only to God. (6:16-18)

Read these passages prayerfully. Use them to reflect on the quality of your own life.

The prayer of St Ignatius

Teach us, good Lord,
to serve you as you deserve;
to give and not to count the cost,
to fight and not to heed the wounds,
to toil and not to seek for rest,
to labour and not to ask for any reward,
save that of knowing that we do your will;
through Jesus Christ our Lord.

Liturgy

Prepare and celebrate a service of Reconciliation (with or without sacramental absolution). Join other catechetical groups for the service. Invite families and other parishioners to join in. The liturgy would include the following elements:

Introduction
Reading
Examination of conscience
Prayers of sorrow
Sign of peace and forgiveness
Form of absolution
Prayers of thanksgiving.

Choose suitable music, hymns and songs.
    Or use the following:

A liturgy on the theme of Reconciliation

SONG

Kyrie Eleison (*More Songs of the Spirit* 197)

INTRODUCTION

Priest   My dear friends, we come together to remember God's love and to celebrate the peace and reconciliation given to us through Jesus. May the grace of our Lord Jesus Christ, the love of God and the fellowship of the holy spirit be with you all.

PRAYER

P   Let us pray.
Father, we come together today to answer the call
you make to us through Jesus your son.
We know that you are love,
and that by living in love we live in you.
We know that you are light
and that by walking in your light we walk with you.
We also recognise that we do not always respond in love,
that we sometimes walk in darkness.
We come together to ask your help,
and to help and support one another.
We are here to seek your healing
and to heal one another.
Through this celebration
make us one with you and with one another.
We ask this through Jesus your Son,
and his Spirit of love and peace
who lives among us for ever and ever.

All   **Amen.**

LITURGY OF THE WORD

Luke 19:1-10 The Story of Zacchaeus, or
Luke 15:11-32 The Story of the forgiving Father.
The Gospel may be mimed or dramatised for greater effect.

HOMILY

SONG

Come back to me (Weston Priory)

ACT OF RECONCILIATION

Reader God calls each of us to be his children. Jesus tells us: I am the vine and you are the branches. A branch cannot bear fruit unless it remains on the vine.

Father, we ask your pardon for the times we have turned away from you – when we have not prayed and thanked you for all the gifts you give us. Lord, have mercy.

All **Christ have mercy.**

God calls us to use our gifts and talents in his service. He calls us freely to choose what is right and good.

Father, we ask your pardon for the times we were lazy and did not use our talents to help others. Lord, have mercy.

A **Christ have mercy.**

God calls us to change our hearts. He wants us to show our love for one another and not be selfish.

Father, we ask pardon for the times we turned away from people who needed our help, especially the lonely, the sick and the old. Lord, have mercy.

A **Christ have mercy.**

God calls us to forgive one another even when we have been hurt and find it hard to forgive.

Father, we ask your pardon for the times we failed to forgive, for the times we bore a grudge or tried to get even with someone. Lord, have mercy.

A **Christ have mercy.**

Jesus calls us to follow him, to follow his example, and the commandments he gave us.

Father, we ask your pardon for the times we failed to act honestly or fairly with other people, and with the things that belonged to them. Lord, have mercy.

A **Christ have mercy.**

Pause for prayer and silent reflection.

A   **I confess to almighty God,**
and to you my brothers and sisters,
that I have sinned through my own fault,
in my thoughts and in my words,
in what I have done and in what I have failed to do.
And I ask blessed Mary ever-virgin,
all the angels and saints,
and you, my brothers and sisters,
to pray for me to the Lord our God.

There may be time now for those who wish to seek individual reconciliation to go to a priest. During this time suitable music or songs may be used. After this, penitents may go to the altar to light a votive candle from the paschal candle.

THE LORD'S PRAYER

THE SIGN OF PEACE

PRAYER

P   Teach us, good Lord,
to serve you as you deserve;
to give and not to count the cost,
to fight and not to heed the wounds,
to toil and not to seek for rest,
to labour and not to ask for any reward,
save that of knowing that we do your will;
through Jesus Christ our Lord.
Amen.

BLESSING

SONG

Though the mountains may fall (*More Songs of the Spirit* 125).

5   Eucharist

In bread we bring you, Lord,
our bodies' labour.
In wine we offer you
our spirit's grief.
We do not ask you, Lord,
who is my neighbour?
but stand united now,
one in belief.
Oh we have gladly heard
your Word, your holy Word,
and now in answer, Lord,
our gifts we bring.
Our selfish hearts make true,
our failing faith renew,
our lives belong to you,
our Lord and King.

The bread we offer you
is blessed and broken,
and it becomes for us
our spirit's food.
Over the cup we bring
your Word is spoken;
make it your gift to us,
your healing blood.
Take all that daily toil
plants in our heart's poor soil,
take all we start and spoil,
each hopeful dream,
the chances we have missed,
the graces we resist,
Lord, in thy Eucharist,
take and redeem.

Kevin Nichols

*I shall drink the new wine with you
in the kingdom of my Father.*

Key ideas

Christian doctrine: that you may understand more fully that in the Eucharist Christ himself is alive and active, feeding and strengthening his faithful people.

Christian living: that you may see that you have a personal responsibility to be involved in the community's celebration.

Prayer and liturgy: that you may plan and celebrate the mystery of the Eucharist so that your involvement leads to a deeper awareness of the power of God's love.

Discussion points

1 'Man by nature enjoys celebrating'. What are the most important occasions and events in your life that you mark with a celebration?
2 Some celebrations are unique, others are repeated. Why is this so?
3 What kind of things do you want to remember by having a celebration?
4 What sort of signs do we use to indicate the importance of the events we celebrate?
5 Celebrations build up our relationships with one another and with God. How important is it to give something of ourselves in a celebration (that is, to make sacrifices)?
6 How much does making sacrifices involve losing our freedom?
7 Why is the idea of a feast often used to describe heaven? How much do ideas about sharing, satisfaction, fullness and completion express the full meaning of the Eucharist?

The word of God

Jesus celebrates his Last Supper

Jesus celebrates the first eucharistic meal

As they were eating, Jesus took some bread, and when he had said the blessing he broke it and gave it to the disciples.

'Take it and eat;' he said 'this is my body.'

Then he took a cup, and when he had returned thanks he gave it to them.

'Drink all of you from this,' he said 'for this is my blood, the blood of the covenant, which is to be poured out for

many for the forgiveness of sins. From now on, I tell you, I
shall not drink wine until the day I drink the new wine with
you in the kingdom of my Father.'

Matthew 26:26-29

1 What message did Jesus intend to convey to us by celebrating the
Last Supper with his disciples?
2 What message do we intend to convey to God and to one another
when we are celebrating the Eucharist?
3 Why does Jesus use the word 'Covenant' to describe this event?

We are united in the Eucharist

The blessing cup that we bless is a communion with the
blood of Christ, and the bread that we break is a communion
with the body of Christ. The fact that there is only one loaf
means that, though there are many of us, we form a single
body because we all have a share in this one loaf.

1 Corinthians 10:16-17

1 Discuss the full meaning of 'communion' in light of this passage.
2 Try to explain how it comes about that 'we, though many, make
one body' in the Eucharist.

The Bread of Life

Then they said to him,
'What must we do if we are to do the works that God
wants?'
Jesus gave them this answer,
'This is working for God; you must believe in the one he
has sent'.
So they said,
'What sign will you give to show us that we should believe
in you? What work will you do? Our fathers had manna to
eat in the desert; as scripture says: He gave them bread from
heaven to eat'.

Jesus answered:

'I tell you most solemnly,
it was not Moses who gave you bread from heaven,
it is my Father who gives you the bread from heaven,
the true bread;
for the bread of God

is that which comes down from heaven
and gives life to the world'.
   'Sir', they said 'give us that bread always'.
   Jesus answered:
   'I am the bread of life
He who comes to me will never be hungry;
he who believes in me will never thirst'.

John 6:28-35

1 Discuss what Jesus meant when he spoke of 'bread which comes down from heaven'.
2 Discuss what Jesus meant when he spoke of 'bread that gives life to the world'.

The teaching of the Church

At the Last Supper, on the night he was betrayed, our Saviour instituted the eucharistic sacrifice of his Body and Blood. This he did in order to perpetuate the sacrifice of the Cross throughout the ages until he should come again, and so to entrust to his beloved Spouse, the Church, a memorial of his death and resurrection: a sacrament of love, a sign of unity, a bond of charity, a paschal banquet in which Christ is consumed, the mind is filled with grace, and a pledge of future glory is given to us.

Vatican II *Constitution on the Sacred Liturgy* 48

1 Why did Jesus celebrate the Last Supper?
2 Which of these phrases do you find most helpful in describing the Eucharist?

Taking part in the celebration

The Church, therefore, earnestly desires that Christ's faithful, when present at this mystery of faith, should not be there as strangers or silent spectators. On the contrary, through a good understanding of the rites and prayers they should take part in the sacred action, conscious of what they are doing with devotion and full collaboration.

They should be instructed by God's word, and be nourished at the table of the Lord's Body. They should give thanks to God. Offering the immaculate victim, not only through the hands of the priest, but also together with him, they should learn to offer themselves.

Through Christ the Mediator, they should be drawn day by day into ever more perfect union with God and each other, so that finally God may be all in all.

Vatican II *Constitution on the Sacred Liturgy* 48

1 Why does the Church say the faithful should not be 'strangers and silent spectators' at Mass?
2 What more do you need to do in order to participate 'knowingly, devoutly and actively'?

Celebrating Sunday

By a tradition handed down from the apostles, which took its origin from the very day of Christ's resurrection, the Church celebrates the paschal mystery every seventh day, which day is appropriately called the Lord's Day or Sunday. For on this day Christ's faithful are bound to come together into one place.

They should listen to the word of God and take part in the Eucharist, thus calling to mind the passion, resurrection, and glory of the Lord Jesus, and giving thanks to God who 'has begotten them again, through the resurrection of Christ from the dead, unto a living hope' (1 Peter 1:3).

The Lord's Day is the original feast day, and it should be proposed to the faithful and taught to them so that it may become in fact a day of joy and of freedom from work.

Other celebrations, unless they be truly of the greatest importance, shall not have precedence over Sunday, which is the foundation and kernel of the whole liturgical year.

Vatican II *Constitution on the Sacred Liturgy* 106

1 Why do we go to Mass on Sunday?
2 What happens when we come together? Think about the ways we:
   hear the word of God
   take part in the Eucharist
   call to mind the passion, death and resurrection of Jesus
   thank God.
3 Suggest ways in which Sunday can really be a 'day of joy and freedom from work'.

Activities

1 Review and explore the structure and meaning of the different parts of the Mass (see above).
2 Trace the themes of reconciliation and peace through the Rite of Mass.
3 Show how and where the Spirit of God works in and through the Eucharist.
4 Illustrate the different themes with posters or collage.
5 Prepare readings and prayers and music for a special celebration of the Eucharist.

Prayer

An Emmaus Prayer

Reader Stay with us, Lord:
behold, evening is coming,
and we still haven't recognised your face
in each of those around us.
All **Stay with us, Lord Jesus Christ.**
Reader Stay with us, Lord:
behold, evening is coming,
and we still haven't shared your bread
in thanksgiving with all who are hungry.
All **Stay with us, Lord Jesus Christ.**

Reader Stay with us, Lord:
  behold, evening is coming,
  and we still haven't recognised your Word
  in the words of those to whom we listen.
All   **Stay with us, Lord Jesus Christ.**
Reader Stay with us, Lord:
  behold, evening is coming,
  and our hearts are still too slow to believe
  that you had to die in order to rise again.
All   **Stay with us, Lord Jesus Christ.**
Reader Stay with us, Lord:
  for our night becomes day
  when you are there.
All   **Stay with us, Lord Jesus Christ.**

The fourth Eucharistic Prayer

Pray and meditate on the fourth Eucharistic Prayer in the Missal.
Note especially that 'He sent the Holy Spirit . . . his first gift to those
who believe' (Baptism).

The Spirit is given to us first in Baptism 'to complete his work on
earth'. The Spirit of Christ works in the world and in each person; the
Eucharist accomplishes our salvation.

'And bring us the fulness of grace'. 'Grace' is the word that describes
our relationship with God. The Eucharist promises to bring us into 'a
state of grace'; it is food for the pilgrim on his journey home.

Liturgy

1 Study the Jewish Passover Meal, perhaps with the help of a Rabbi
   or a Jewish family. (See *Passover Haggadah* by M. Lehmann,
   published by Lehmann, Gateshead.)
2 Prepare for and celebrate a form of the Passover Meal.
3 Study the liturgy for Maundy Thursday. If the time is appropriate,
   prepare to celebrate this feast of the Institution of the Eucharist.
4 Prepare for and celebrate a house-Mass for candidates, parents,
   catechists and their families; or use the following:

A liturgy on the theme of the Eucharist

SONG

Come and Worship (*Songs of the Spirit* 34)

READING

Exodus 12:1-14

SONG

When Israel was in Egypt's Land (*Hymns Old and New* 609)

A MEAL TO REMEMBER

Narra-tor 1: During the unhappy time when the Israelites were living in slavery in Egypt, a ray of hope shone through their suffering – the knowledge that they were God's Chosen People and that one day he would rescue them. This he did through the person of Moses who went to Egypt and persuaded the Pharaoh to let his people go.

It became tradition for the Jewish people to have a celebration meal each year in remembrance of God's goodness to them. It was eaten at the Feast of Passover and was called a 'Meal to Remember'.

Narra-tor 2: The days before the Passover were busy ones for the Jewish housewife. She cleaned her house from top to bottom and she also had to bake the special unleavened bread and prepare other special foods.

Narra-tor 3: On the evening of the Passover the men went to the service at the Synagogue. While they were away she set the table using her finest white cloth.
White cloth is placed on the table.
On this were placed two candlesticks; a large round dish containing three pieces of unleavened bread; a large wine glass or goblet; a bowl of salt to represent the tears of suffering in the land of Egypt; a dish of bitter herbs to remind them of the bitterness of slavery; some haroseth (a mixture of stewed apples, wine and nuts) to represent the clay or mortar

for the bricks; a shank bone was used in place of the paschal lamb; and cinnamon sticks took the place of straw.

Narra-
tor 4: Through this ceremony the Jewish children learned about the history of their ancestors and how God answered their pleas for mercy.

SONG

Lord, have mercy (*Hymns Old and New* 323)

Narra-
tor 5: The men return from their evening prayers and take their places for the Feast. The seat of honour is taken by the eldest man, the father, who is called the President of the Feast.

Presid-
ent: Blessed are you Lord, God of all creation, through your goodness we have this wine to offer, fruit of the vine.

The cup is passed round. Each person says **Amen** *as he or she receives the cup.*

Youn-
gest
Boy: Why is this night different from all other nights?

On other nights we may eat either leavened or unleavened bread, but on this night only unleavened bread?

Why on all other nights may we eat other kinds of herbs, but on this night only bitter herbs?

Presid-
ent: This is the BREAD of sorrow that our fathers ate in the land of Egypt. We eat unleavened bread on this night because our ancestors left Egypt in such haste that there was no time for them to wait until their dough was leavened.

We eat BITTER HERBS on this night because the Egyptians made bitter the lives of our fathers with hard service.

We eat the paschal or PASSOVER LAMB on this night because God in his mercy passed over the houses of our fathers in Egypt but destroyed the first born of the Egyptians.

The President blesses the bread and distributes it.
Blessed are you Lord, God of all creation, through your goodness we have this bread to offer which earth has given.

As the bread is shared, each person says **Amen.**

Speak praises to God to whom belongs what we have eaten.

All: **Praise we our God for the food we have eaten.**

SONG

Alleluia Alleluia (*More Songs of the Spirit* 190)

Narra- The Last Supper was intended to be:

tor 6: a farewell meal where Jesus said Goodbye to his friends,

a memorial of Jesus; he asked his friends, the Apostles to go on doing this in memory of him,

a sacrifice – a way of keeping his promise to feed the world with his own body and blood.

GOSPEL

Matthew 26:17-20, 26-30

HOMILY

BIDDING PRAYERS

On this night when Jesus gave a new commandment of love and service, draw attention to the service given by members of the group, e.g. nursing, teaching, visiting the sick, etc. Compose prayers related to these tasks and to the mission of all disciples.

LITURGY OF THE EUCHARIST

SONG

In bread we bring you (*Celebration Hymnal* 135)

PRAYER OVER THE GIFTS

P   Lord make us worthy to celebrate these mysteries. Each time we offer this memorial sacrifice the work of our redemption is accomplished. We make our prayer through Christ our Lord.

A   **Amen.**

COMMUNION SONG

Only a shadow (*More Songs of the Spirit* 131)

PRAYER AFTER COMMUNION

P   Almighty God,
we receive new life
from the supper your Son gave us in this world.
May we find full contentment
in the meal we hope to share
in your eternal kingdom.
We ask this through Christ our Lord.
Amen.

SONG

We are the Easter People (*More Songs of the Spirit* 108)

Be sealed with the gift
of the Holy Spirit.

6 Confirmation

O gracious and holy Father,
give us wisdom to perceive you,
intelligence to understand you,
diligence to seek you,
patience to wait for you,
eyes to behold you,
a heart to meditate upon you,
and a life to proclaim you;
through the power of the Spirit
of Jesus Christ our Lord.

St Benedict

Key ideas

Christian doctrine: that you may understand that the sacrament of Confirmation completes your initiation into the Church through your own personal experience of Pentecost.

Christian living: that you may see that through this sacrament you show the concern and love of Jesus himself who was priest, prophet and king.

Prayer and liturgy: that you may experience the sacrament of Confirmation as a celebration of the faith of the whole community guided by the Holy Spirit.

Discussion points

1 Who is the Holy Spirit?
2 Where do we see the Holy Spirit present and active in the world?
3 What do we mean by the phrase 'by their fruits you shall know them'?
4 What does God tell us the Holy Spirit will do for us? See John 14:26-27, 15:15-16.
5 What do you want the Holy Spirit to do for you, for the world?
6 What do the symbols of oil, fire and wind tell us about the Holy Spirit?

The word of God
The gifts of the Spirit
The coming of the 'virtuous king'

A shoot springs from the stock of Jesse,
a scion thrusts from his roots:
on him the spirit of the Lord rests,
a spirit of wisdom and insight,
a spirit of counsel and power,
a spirit of knowledge and the fear of the Lord,
(The fear of the Lord is his breath.)
He does not judge by appearances,
he gives no verdict on hearsay,
but judges the wretched with integrity,
and with equity gives a verdict for the poor of the land.

Isaiah 11:1-4

These are the gifts God promised to the 'virtuous king'. The same gifts are passed on by Jesus, through his death and resurrection, to us in the sacrament of Confirmation.

A Mission of the prophet

The spirit of the Lord has been given to me
for the Lord has anointed me.
He has sent me to bring good news to the poor,
to bind up hearts that are broken;
to proclaim liberty to captives,
freedom to those in prison;
to proclaim a year of favour from the Lord.

Isaiah 61:1-2

The Spirit given to Jesus is the same as that given to us in the sacrament of Confirmation.

St Paul on the Spirit in the Church

Now you together are Christ's body: but each of you is a different part of it. In the Church, God has given the first place to apostles, the second to prophets, the third to teachers, after them miracles, and after them the gift of healing; helpers, good leaders, those with many languages.

Are all of them apostles or all of them prophets, or all of them teachers? Do they all have the gift of miracles, or all have the gift of healing? Do all speak strange languages and do all interpret them?

1 Corinthians 12:27-30

St Paul lists some of the gifts given to the Church. Each of us has his or her own particular gift for use in God's service.

The Christian life

The whole of the Law is summarised in a single command:

Love your neighbour as yourself. If you go snapping at each other and tearing each other to pieces, you had better watch or you will destroy the whole community.

Let me put it like this: if you are guided by the Spirit you will be in no danger of yielding to self-indulgence, since self-indulgence is the opposite of the Spirit. The Spirit is totally against such a thing, and it is precisely because the two are so opposed that you do not always carry out your good intentions. If you are led by the Spirit, no law can touch you.

When self-indulgence is at work the results are obvious: fornication, gross indecency and sexual irresponsibility; idolatry and sorcery; feuds and wrangling, jealousy, bad temper and quarrels; disagreements, factions, envy, drunkenness, orgies and similar things. I warn you now, as I warned you before; those who behave like this will not inherit the kingdom of God.

What the Spirit brings is very different: love, joy, peace, patience, kindness, goodness, trustfulness, gentleness and self-control.

There can be no law against things like that, of course. You cannot belong to Christ Jesus unless you crucify all self-indulgent passions and desires. Since the Spirit is our life, let us be directed by the Spirit. We must stop being conceited, provocative and envious.

Galatians 5:14-26

We see the fruits of the Spirit in the lives of those who choose to allow the Spirit to direct their lives.

The teaching of the Church
'More like Christ – priest, prophet and king'

Priest

Incorporated into the Church through baptism, the faithful
are consecrated by the baptismal character to the exercise of
the cult of the Christian religion.

Reborn as sons of God, they must confess before men the
faith which they have received from God through the
Church.

Bound more intimately to the Church by the sacrament of
confirmation, they are endowed by the Holy Spirit with
special strength.

Hence they are more strictly obliged to spread and defend
the faith both by word and by deed as true witnesses of
Christ.

Vatican II *Constitution on the Church* 11

We are consecrated to the service of God in Confirmation and
therefore:

We are bound more intimately to the Church.
The Holy Spirit gives us special strength.
We are more strictly obliged to spread and defend the faith.

In what ways can we imitate Christ in his priestly role?

Prophet

The holy People of God shares also in Christ's prophetic
office. It spreads abroad a living witness to him, especially by
means of a life of faith and charity and by offering to God a
sacrifice of praise, the tribute of lips which give honour to
his name (see Hebrews 13:15).

Vatican II *Constitution on the Church* 12

The mark of the prophet is to be a living witness to Jesus:
by means of a life of faith and charity, and
by offering God a sacrifice of praise.
In what practical ways can we be living witnesses to Jesus?

King

All men are called to belong to the new People of God.

Wherefore this People, while remaining one and unique, is to be spread throughout the whole world and must exist in all ages, so that the purpose of God's will may be fulfilled.

In the beginning God made human nature one. After his children were scattered, he decreed that they should at length be unified again (cf. Jn 11:52).

It was for this reason that God sent his son, whom he appointed heir of all things (cf. Heb 1:2), that he might be Teacher, King and Priest of all, the Head of the new and universal people of the sons of God.

For this God finally sent his Son's Spirit as Lord and Lifegiver. He it is who, on behalf of the whole Church and each and every one of those who believe, is the principle of their coming and remaining together in the teaching of the apostles and in fellowship, in the breaking of bread and in prayers (Acts 2:42).

Vatican II *Constitution on the Church* 13

God sent his Son to be the Head of the new and universal people. Jesus is not a king in the ordinary sense. He came among us as one who serves.

How can we help to bring about his kingdom through our service of God and of others?

Pope John Paul II at Coventry

'Baptism of itself, is only a beginning, a point of departure ... ' the Pope had said at Westminster. He told the newly-confirmed at Coventry that they were 'full citizens now of the People of God'.

'The Sponsor who stands at your side represents for you the whole Community ... '

Suggest ways in which a parish might be encouraged:
to show the newly confirmed that they have a special place in it;
to invite them to play a more active role in meeting the needs of the Community;
to encourage them, in their own way, to witness to the truth of the Gospel.

'You will hear the words of the Church spoken over you, calling upon the Spirit:

> to confirm your faith,
> to seal you in his love,
> to strengthen you for his service'.

Reflect on these three actions of the Spirit and share your understanding of them with the group.

He told the newly-confirmed: 'Together with all the confirmed, you will become living stones in the Cathedral of peace. Indeed you are called by God to be instruments of his peace'.

How would you encourage the newly-confirmed of the parish to respond to this call 'to be instruments of his peace'?

WHERE THE SPIRIT OF THE LORD IS,

THERE IS FREEDOM

Activities

1 Show by poster, collage, mime or drama, some of the ways that we can see the Holy Spirit at work.
2 List the gifts of the Holy Spirit. Write a prayer asking for the gifts you would particularly like to receive. Think about ways in which you would use these gifts to build up the Church and the Kingdom of God.
3 Watch on video the homily of Pope John Paul II at Coventry and the Rite of Confirmation which follows.

4 Look up some Scripture texts about the Holy Spirit and write a
sentence telling what the passage says.

Genesis 1:1-2   John 14:16-17
Genesis 2:7   John 19:30
Ezechiel 37:1-14   Acts 2:1-4
Joel 3:1-2   Acts 2:32-33
Luke 1:26-35   Romans 5:5
Matthew 3:13-17   1 Corinthians 12:4-11

Prayer

'I am a link in a chain'

God has created me to do him
some definite service;
He has committed some work to me
which he has not committed to another.
I have my mission – I may never know it in this life,
                           but I shall be told it in the next.
Somehow I am necessary for his purposes.
I have a great part in his work;

I am a link in a chain,
a bond of connection between persons.
He has not created me for nothing.
I shall do good, I shall do his work;
I shall be an angel of peace, a preacher of truth
in my own place, while not intending it,
if I do but keep his commandments
and serve him in my calling.

Therefore, I will trust him.
Whatever, wherever I am,

I can never be thrown away.
If I am in sickness, my sickness may serve him;
if I am in sorrow, my sorrow may serve him.
My sickness or perplexity or sorrow
may be necessary causes of some great end,
which is quite beyond us.
He does nothing in vain;
He may prolong life, he may shorten it;

He knows what he is about.
    John Henry Newman, from *Meditations on Christian Doctrine*

The liturgy of Confirmation

Study the prayers of the Rite of Confirmation

OPENING PRAYER

Lord, fulfil your promise.
Send your Holy Spirit
to make us witnesses before the world
to the good news proclaimed by Jesus Christ our Lord
who lives and reigns
with you and the Holy Spirit,
one God, for ever and ever. Amen.

After the Readings, the Bishop speaks about the meaning of the sacrament.

PRESENTATION OF THE CANDIDATES

The candidates stand up in turn when a priest calls their names.

RENEWAL OF BAPTISMAL PROMISES

Bishop Do you reject Satan and all his works and all his empty promises?

Candidates **I do.**

Bishop Do you believe in God the Father Almighty,
    Creator of heaven and earth?

Candidates **I do.**

Bishop Do you believe in Jesus Christ
    his only Son, our Lord,
    who was born of the virgin Mary,
    was crucified, died and was buried,
    rose from the dead,
    and is now seated at the right hand
    of the Father?

Candi- **I do.**
dates

Bishop Do you believe in the Holy Spirit,
the Lord, the giver of life,
who came upon the Apostles at
Pentecost and today is given to you
sacramentally in Confirmation?
Candi- **I do.**
dates

Bishop Do you believe in the Holy
Catholic Church,
the communion of saints,
the forgiveness of sins,
the resurrection of the body,
and life everlasting?
Candi- **I do.**
dates

Bishop This is our faith.
This is the faith of the Church.
We are proud to profess it
in Christ Jesus our Lord.
All **Amen.**

THE PRAYER OF CONSECRATION

Bishop My dear friends:
in baptism God our Father gave
the new birth of eternal life
to his chosen sons and daughters.
Let us pray to our Father
that he will pour out the Holy Spirit
to strengthen his sons and daughters
with his gifts
and anoint them
to be more like Christ the Son of God.

The Bishop and priests extend their hands over the candidates.

Bishop All powerful God,
Father of our Lord Jesus Christ,

by water and the Holy Spirit
you freed your sons and daughters from sin
and gave them new life.
Send your Holy Spirit upon them
to be their Helper and Guide.
Give them
the spirit of wisdom and understanding,
the spirit of right judgement and courage,
the spirit of knowledge and reverence.
Fill them
with the spirit of wonder and awe
in your presence.
We ask this through Christ our Lord.

All   **Amen.**

THE ANOINTING WITH CHRISM

The oil of Chrism is presented to the Bishop. The candidates and their sponsors approach the Bishop. The Bishop makes the sign of the cross with chrism on the candidate's forehead and the sponsor places his or her hand on the candidate's shoulder.

Bishop N . . . . , be sealed with the gift of the Holy Spirit.
The newly confirmed   **Amen.**
Bishop Peace be with you.
The newly confirmed   **And also with you.**

BIDDING PRAYERS

PRAYER OVER THE GIFTS

Priest   Lord,
we celebrate the memorial of our redemption
by which your Son won for us the gift of the
Holy Spirit.
Accept our offerings,
and send us your Holy Spirit
to make us more like Christ
in bearing witness to the world.
We make this prayer through Christ our Lord. Amen.

When Eucharistic Prayer 1 is used, the special form of 'Father, accept this offering' *is said:*

Father, accept this offering
from your whole family
and from those reborn in Baptism
and confirmed by the coming of the Holy Spirit.
Protect them with your love and keep them close to you.

PRAYER AFTER COMMUNION

Priest Lord,
help those you have anointed by your Spirit
and fed with the body and blood of your Son.
Support them through every trial
and by their works of love
build up the Church in holiness and joy.
We make this prayer through Christ our Lord. Amen.

A liturgy of preparation for Confirmation

SONG

The light of Christ (*Songs of the Spirit* 60; *Celebration Hymnal* 653)

INTRODUCTION

Priest In this celebration we think of the day for Confirmation which is close at hand. We remember how God calls us out of darkness into the light. The light is his word and the example of our lives reflecting his word to those we meet.

SOLEMN LIGHTING OF THE PASCHAL CANDLE

P Dear friends in Christ,
we share in the light of God's glory
through his Son, the light of the world.
Let us listen to his word
and celebrate the mystery of his love,
then we may be confident
that we shall share his victory over death
and live with him for ever in God.

Christ yesterday and today
the beginning and the end
Alpha and Omega
all time belongs to him
and all the ages
to him be glory and power
through every age for ever.

All **Amen.**
P By his holy and glorious wounds
may Christ our Lord guard us and keep us.
A **Amen.**
P May the light of Christ, rising in glory,
dispel the darkness of our hearts and minds. Amen.
A **Amen.**

(Celebrant lights the candle)

PRAYER

P   Let us pray that the Spirit will work through our lives
      to bring Christ to the world.
      Father of light,
      let the Spirit you sent on your Church
      to begin the teaching of the gospel
      continue to work in the world
      through the hearts of those who believe.
      We ask this through Christ our Lord.
A   **Amen.**

LITURGY OF THE WORD

READING

1 John 1:5-7
Psalm 26:1, 4, 8b-9abc, 13-14

RESPONSE

A   **The Lord is my light and my help.**

GOSPEL

Matthew 5:14-16

HOMILY

*(After the homily, the parents or sponsor come forward and take the
candidate's baptismal candle or some other suitable candle and light it
from the paschal candle. It is then given to the candidate with the
words*: 'Receive the light of Christ.')

INTERCESSIONS

P   Let us pray to the Lord that he will guide us and sustain us as
         we seek to serve him and one another.
Reader   By your coming as man,
A   **Lord save your people.**
R   By the words of your teaching,
A   **Give us wisdom.**
R   By the signs that you worked,
A   **Strengthen our faith.**
R   By your suffering and death,

A	**Free us from our sins.**
R	By your rising to new life,
A	**Give us a new heart.**
R	By the sending of your holy Spirit,
A	**Give us hope and joy.**
P	God of unchanging power and light,
	look with favour and mercy on your entire Church.
	Bring lasting salvation to mankind,
	so that the world may see
	the fallen lifted up,
	the old made new,
	and all things brought to perfection,
	through him who is their origin,
	our Lord Jesus Christ,
	who lives and reigns for ever and ever.
	Amen.

LITURGY OF THE EUCHARIST

SONG

Father in my life I see (*More Songs of the Spirit* 144)

PRAYER OVER THE OFFERINGS

P	Lord, send your Spirit on these gifts and through them help the Church you love to show your salvation to all the world. We ask this in the name of Jesus Christ our Lord.
A	**Amen.**

COMMUNION SONG

I will be with you (*Songs of the Spirit* 45)

PRAYER AFTER COMMUNION

P	Lord, through this eucharist send the Holy Spirit of Pentecost into our hearts to keep us always in your love. We ask this through Christ our Lord.
A	**Amen.**

SONG

If God is for us (*Songs of the Spirit* 64)

As the Father sent me
so am I sending you.

7 Mission

Discover yourself

'Every person must have a concern for self, and feel a responsibility to discover his mission in life. God has given each normal person a capacity to achieve some end. True, some are endowed with more talent than others, but God has left none of us talentless. Potential powers of creativity are within us, and we have the duty to work assiduously to discover these powers.'

Martin Luther King

Key ideas

Christian doctrine: that you may know that as fully initiated members of the Church, you share in the mission of Christ himself to the world.

Christian living: that you may accept and value your responsibility to preach the gospel to all people.

Prayer and liturgy: that you may pray and reflect on your mission particularly in sharing with the poor, working for peace and serving those in need.

Discussion points

1 Describe the experience of being confirmed – the ceremony, the celebration. Say how you feel about it now.
2 How do you feel you can live your Christian life more fully? Use the following list to see how you can be 'more like Christ, the Son of God'.

   Prayer

I have an awareness of God's role in my life. I am open to the guidance of the Holy Spirit.

Mass – Liturgy of the Church

I am committed to celebrating with the Church on Sundays and holy days. I want to contribute to the celebration by praying, listening and praising God.

Moral and personal life

I have a desire to keep God's commandments and make my daily decisions according to God's will. I examine my life daily and celebrate regularly the sacrament of reconciliation.

Service

I am generous with my time and aware of the needs of those around me. I am willing to use my talents, especially for the lonely, the needy and the aged.

Further religious education

I understand the basic principles of my faith. I recognise my need to continue studying my faith all through my life.

The word of God
The mission of Jesus

Peter speaks to the Christians in the house of Cornelius

Then Peter addressed them:
'The truth I have now come to realise' he said 'is that God does not have favourites, but that anybody of any nationality who fears God and does what is right is acceptable to him.

'It is true, God sent his word to the people of Israel, and it was to them that the good news of peace was brought by Jesus Christ – but Jesus is Lord of all men. You must have heard about the recent happenings in Judea, about Jesus of Nazareth and how he began in Galilee, after John had been preaching baptism. God had anointed him with the Holy Spirit and with power, and because God was with him, Jesus went about doing good and curing all who had fallen into the power of the devil.'

Acts 10:34-38

1 What truths have you come to realise through the Confirmation programme and through the experience of being confirmed?

2 You have been anointed with the Holy Spirit. How do you propose to 'go about doing good and curing all who have fallen into the power of the devil'?

The mission of the disciples

Jesus appears to the disciples

In the evening of that same day, the first day of the week, the doors were closed in the room where the disciples were, for fear of the Jews. Jesus came and stood among them. He said to them,

'Peace be with you',

and showed them his hands and his side.

The disciples were filled with joy when they saw the Lord, and he said to them again,

'Peace be with you.

'As the Father sent me,
so am I sending you.'

After saying this he breathed on them and said:

'Receive the Holy Spirit.
For those whose sins you forgive,
they are forgiven;
for those whose sins you retain,
they are retained.'

John 20:19-23

1 Where can you share the peace that is God's gift to you?
2 To whom is God sending you on a mission?
3 In what ways can you forgive and retain the sins of others?

The mission to the world

Jesus appears to the disciples in Galilee

Meanwhile the eleven disciples set out for Galilee, to the mountain where Jesus had arranged to meet them. When they saw him they fell down before him, though some hesitated. Jesus came up and spoke to them. He said,

'All authority in heaven and on earth has been given to me.

Go, therefore, make disciples of all the nations; baptise them in the name of the Father and of the Son and of the Holy Spirit, and teach them to observe all the commands I gave you. And know that I am with you always; yes, to the end of time.'

Matthew 28:16-20

Notice how people are first to be evangelised (make disciples) then to come to the sacraments (baptise) and finally to learn to live more deeply the Christian life (teach).

The life of the disciple

Paul calls the Ephesians to unite

I, the prisoner in the Lord, implore you therefore to lead a life worthy of your vocation. Bear with one another charitably, in complete selflessness, gentleness and patience.

Do all you can to preserve the unity of the Spirit by the peace that binds you together.

There is one Body, one Spirit, just as you were all called into one and the same hope when you were called.

There is one Lord, one faith, one baptism, and one God who is Father of all, over all, through all and within all.

Ephesians 4:1-6

1 What are the things you have to do to be worthy of your vocation?
2 Why do you think that Paul says that unity is so important?

Not the end, but the beginning

As you see, I do not want to make it only a passing visit to you and I hope to spend some time with you, the Lord permitting. In any case, I shall be staying at Ephesus until Pentecost because a big and important door has opened for my work and there is a great deal of opposition.

1 Corinthians 16:7-9

1 Has a big and important door opened for you?
2 What opposition are you likely to encounter on your mission?

The teaching of the Church

Lay people in the Church

In the Church, there is a diversity of service but unity of purpose. Christ conferred on the apostles and their successors the duty of teaching, sanctifying, and ruling in His name and power.

But the laity, too, share in the priestly, prophetic, and royal office of Christ and therefore have their own role to play in the mission of the whole People of God in the Church and in the world.

They exercise a genuine apostolate by their activity on behalf of bringing the gospel and holiness to men, and on behalf of penetrating and perfecting the temporal sphere of things through the spirit of the gospel. In this way, their temporal activity can openly bear witness to Christ and promote the salvation of men.

Since it is proper to the layman's state in life for him to spend his days in the midst of the world and of secular transactions, he is called by God to burn with the spirit of Christ and to exercise his apostolate in the world as a kind of leaven.

Vatican II *Decree on the Laity* 2

1 How will you bring 'the gospel and holiness to men'?
2 How will you 'penetrate and perfect the temporal sphere of things through the spirit of the gospel'?
3 What do the bishops mean when they say 'to burn with the spirit of Christ' and 'a kind of leaven'?

Living in union with Christ

Since Christ in His mission from the Father is the fountain and source of the whole apostolate of the Church, the success of the lay apostolate depends upon the laity's living union with Christ. For the Lord has said, 'He who abides in me, and I in him, he bears much fruit: for without me you can do nothing' (Jn 15:5).

This life of intimate union with Christ in the Church is nourished by spiritual aids which are common to all faithful, especially active participation in the sacred liturgy. These are to be used by the laity in such a way that while properly fulfilling their secular duties in the ordinary conditions of life, they do not disassociate union with Christ from that life. Rather, by performing their work according to God's will they can grow in that union.

In this way must the laity make progress in holiness, showing a ready and happy spirit, and trying prudently and patiently to overcome difficulties. Neither family concerns nor other secular affairs should be excluded from their religious programme of life. For as the Apostle states, 'Whatever you do in word or work, do all in the name of the Lord Jesus Christ, giving thanks to God the Father through him'. (Col. 3:17). Such a life requires a continual exercise of faith, hope and charity.

Vatican II *Decree on the Laity* 4

1 How can you foster a 'living union with Christ'?
2 What can you do to ensure that you do not separate this 'union with Christ' from 'the ordinary conditions of life'?
3 How can you make progress in holiness?

Activities

1 Plan an activity which will benefit someone in your parish, school or community.
2 Plan how you might help future candidates for Confirmation by
   improvements to the parish programme
   joining some kind of meeting or discussion
   some other help with the programme.
3 Desert Island Discs: bring a record which has a message for you; play it and say why you would take it on a desert island.
4 Organise a panel by inviting confirmed Christians and others to examine and question their faith and beliefs.
5 Show slides or photos that have a message for you and invite others to comment.

Prayer

The prayer of St Francis

Lord, make me an instrument of your peace.
where there is hatred, let me sow love;
where there is injury, pardon;
where there is discord, union;
where there is doubt, faith;
where there is despair, hope;
where there is darkness, light;
where there is sadness, joy.

O divine Master,
grant that we may not so much seek
to be consoled as to console;
to be understood as to understand;
to be loved as to love;
through the love of your Son who died for us,
Jesus Christ our Lord.

Liturgy

1 Celebrate a Mass of thanksgiving in the Parish with a presentation of Certificates.
2 Plan some social event to follow the liturgy.
3 Alternatively celebrate the following:

A liturgy on the theme of mission

SONG

Be like your Father (*More Songs of the Spirit* 176)

INTRODUCTION

Priest   We welcome today our brothers and sisters in Christ who have recently received the sacrament of Confirmation. We give thanks to God for the gift of the Spirit so generously poured out on them. We pray for them and their families that God's Spirit may bring them peace and joy.

PENITENTIAL RITE

P   Lord Jesus, you came to gather the nations into the peace of God's kingdom: Lord, have mercy.

All   **Lord, have mercy.**

P   You come in word and sacrament to strengthen us in holiness: Christ, have mercy.

A   **Christ, have mercy.**

P   You will come in glory with salvation for your people: Lord, have mercy.

A   **Lord, have mercy.**

P   May almighty God have mercy on us, forgive us our sins and bring us to everlasting life. Amen.

A   **Amen.**

PRAYER

P   Let us pray.
      God our Father,
      you will all men to be saved
      and come to the knowledge of your truth.
      Send workers into your great harvest
      that the gospel may be preached to every creature;
      and your people, gathered together by the word of life
      and strengthened by the power of the sacraments,
      may advance in the way of salvation and love.
      We ask this through Christ our Lord.

A   **Amen.**

LITURGY OF THE WORD

READING

Romans 12:4-13

SONG

Be not afraid (*More Songs of the Spirit* 196)

GOSPEL

Matthew 28:16-20

HOMILY

The Bidding prayers and the Offertory procession may be linked. The newly confirmed may represent the lives and the work of local saints by symbols, banners or posters. They may also show the life and ministry of those in the local community who carry out the mission of Christ today. Each presentation may be accompanied by a suitable bidding prayer.

At the end of the procession the gifts of bread and wine are brought up with the Confirmation Certificates if they are to be presented at the end of the Liturgy.

LITURGY OF THE EUCHARIST

SONG

I give my hands (*Hymns Old and New* 235)

PRAYER OVER THE GIFTS

P   Lord, look upon the face of Christ your Son
who gave up his life to set all men free.
Through him may your name be praised
among all peoples from East to West,
and everywhere may one sacrifice be offered
to give you glory.
We ask this through Christ our Lord.

A   **Amen.**

COMMUNION SONG

Walk humbly with your God (*More Songs of the Spirit* 171)

PRAYER AFTER COMMUNION

P   Lord, you renew our life with this gift of redemption. Through this help to eternal salvation may the true faith continue to grow throughout the world. We ask this through Christ our Lord.

A   **Amen.**
The newly-confirmed are now called forward by name and presented with their certificates. The Celebrant may say to each of them: 'Go in peace to love and serve the Lord'.

SONG

Follow me (*Songs of the Spirit* 73).

My journey in faith

NAME..

BORN...........day of ....19...........

FATHER...

MOTHER............. ....

BAPTISED..........day of ....19..........

BY...

AT..

GODFATHER...

GODMOTHER...

RECEIVED FIRST HOLY COMMUNION

AT ....

ON ....day of ....19...........

CELEBRANT...

ENROLLED AS A CANDIDATE FOR
CONFIRMATION

ON ....day of ....19...........

AT ....

BY...

CONFIRMED

AT ....

ON ....day of . ...19..........

BY...

SPONSOR ....